Surviving the Fires of Sorrow

A Family's Journey of Suffering and Loss
Leads to Deeper Trust

By Mitch A. Schultz

Mitch A. Schultz

Dedication

Dedicated to the memory of our son
Travis Andrew Schultz
Born: November 19, 1986
Died: August 22, 1999
HE LIVED A BRIEF BUT FULL LIFE!

Dedicated also to my precious daughter, Breanna (Breezy). While this book does not tell your story, your constant patience, your stable support, and your deep faith in Jesus became a tremendous source of strength for me. In truth, I am glad I never had to devote a full section of this book to your life. Perhaps you were spared because God knew I could not walk through these fires alone.

*****

"God, I pray thee, light these idle sticks of my life, that I may burn for thee. Consume my life, for it is thine. I seek not long life, but a full one for you, Lord Jesus." – Jim Elliot

"You always know the man who has been through the *fires of sorrow*. You are certain you can go to him in trouble and find that he has ample leisure for you. If a man has not been through the *fires of sorrow*, he is apt to be contemptuous; he has no time for you. If you receive yourself in the fires of sorrow, God will make you nourishment for other people." – Oswald Chambers[1]

---

[1] Oswald Chambers, *My Utmost for His Highest*, rev. ed. (Nashville: Thomas Nelson, 1992), June 25.

Surviving the Fires of Sorrow

I want to thank Svenja Miner for taking on the unreasonable task of taking an out of print book and typing all 58,222 words on her computer so we would have an electronic version of the original. Your work, Svenja, was worth far more than the pithy fifty cents a page I gave you. Thank you, and we are so glad you are part of this family.

Contents

Introduction

Part 1 Elaine's Story
1. Not the Trip We'd Planned!
2. A Pledge for Life!
3. A Revisit to Childhood Pain!
4. Painful Lessons!
5. Where is God in All of This?
6. The World as Seen from a Waiting Room
7. An Expression of True Commitment
8. Ministry at Arm's Length
9. Praying for the Boy in Mexico
10. This Side of Healing
11. A Cruel Game of Waiting!
12. God's Precious Child
13. Watching God Move
14. The Fires of Sorrow
15. Coming to Terms with Change

Part 2 Travis's Story
16. Uncertain Days
17. The Beginning of Another Trial
18. Broken Windows
19. At Wit's End
20. Watching God Move Again
21. God, What Are You Doing?
22. Unexpected Bends
23. Preparing for a Battle
24. The Letter I Never Wanted to Write
25. Funeral Plans, Before Death
26. Facing Death

27. I'll See You There, Son
28. No Postcards from Heaven
29. As Free as a Butterfly
30. Life Goes On
31. Motivation to Move On
32. Thankfulness for the Grace of Endurance

Part 3 Brett and Us Since
33. A Movie, Breanna, and It's Time for a Change!
34. Not Again! - Not You, Brett!
35. A Turn for the Better
36. Settling, Finally!
37. Sorrow No More!

Introduction

Eighteen years and more have passed since the events described in this book. I am far from the man I was when I first wrote this, but I desire to change very little of what you read. The events happened, and while I've changed, hopefully for the better, I cannot change the past. There is no doubt I would write this story differently if I wrote it now, but I do like looking back and seeing how in my youth and vulnerability I still had so far to go. If these events happened to me now, I am not sure I could handle it as well as I did then. I believe that God's sovereignty tested me relative to who I was and what I could handle. I am thankful He trusted me with this suffering but also thankful that He knows my thresholds.

I've added a section to the end of this book about some of the events surrounding my youngest son's bout with lymphoma cancer, along with filling in some of the gaps of these past eighteen years.

Finally, as you prepare to dive in, I realize that some people have concluded that God doesn't really care about them. Situations like those I want to share with you in this book have, undoubtedly, contributed to their perception of God. When good people experience bad things, it is difficult for them to maintain that God is good and loving.

I want to tell you, however, that our trials strengthened rather than weakened our faith in Jesus. It wasn't easy for us to reach that conclusion because we, too, have had to trust that what God was doing was right and good, even though our myopic view of things seemed to suggest otherwise. Convinced that God is sovereign, even over suffering, provided for us a safe place to rest when the storms blew strongest.

Mitch A Schultz
mitchschultz@me.com
www.beforeyouquit.us
www.fruitfulvineministry.com

Part 1

Elaine's Story

It was a warm afternoon. As we stood together at a spot overlooking a beautiful lake near our home in northeast Georgia, Elaine nestled her head on my shoulder and reflected on the first day that she met me nearly twenty years earlier, not far from where we were then standing.

"Are you still glad we got married?" I asked.

"Yes," came her quick reply. She still struggled to speak and in her own way said something to the effect of, "But would *you* have done it differently if you had known what we have had to go through?"

Without a pause, I pulled her close to me and assured her, as I often do, "Elaine, if God would have forewarned us with every detail of all that would happen to you and to our son Travis, I would have done the very same thing." She smiled, and we resumed our quiet reflection in that idyllic place overlooking the lake.

The events about which I write really began on July 23, 1983. The moment my wife and I pledged our devotion to each other in marriage, we committed our lives to the Lord for Him to do with us as He pleased. It was in that expression of covenant love that we agreed to accept sickness when we preferred health, poverty when we would not have turned down wealth, and turmoil when we would have much desired peace.

Later, when Elaine was being operated on and fighting for her life on June 6, 1998, the surgeon came to tell me that she had little chance of surviving. When someone hears such words, the waiting room becomes his only world. There in that confine, I found myself pacing, praying, and making phone calls to solicit as much prayer support as possible. As I sat there, I found myself drifting in time and remembering the words that I had said at an altar at the front of a church nearly fifteen years earlier. The power and significance of those words suddenly took on meaning as never before. While we longed that our lives together would be filled with happiness and uninterrupted joy, this is not the way it has turned out for us.

We say such words so routinely at weddings. I remember listening to the pastor as he guided me through those ritualistic statements and thinking, *Would you just get on with it? I want to kiss her.* But now I found myself beginning to place new significance in and give new relevance to those words. There in the hospital lounge, those words suddenly meant something, and they resurfaced from the deep memory bank of my mind to become a beacon for what would turn out to be a very dark path.

"Mitch, will you love and cherish Elaine for better, for worse, for richer, for poorer, in sickness, and in health?"

Right there before God, I vowed, *Lord, whatever you have in mind for Elaine, I want to say right now, I accept it. If you want her, you can take her. If you keep her here, and she needs help, I will help her.* You see, when I married Elaine and said those vital words before God, we both committed our lives to serve Him, and we were saying, "God, you are invited to do whatever you want with us." It was a pledge to serve God together, not simply to serve each other or to fulfill personal happiness through a relationship with that person. God had brought us together so that we would be useful to Him together, not alone. We were finding that how He carries this out is up to Him, and sometimes it will be in ways that we would not have chosen.

In loss, the pain runs deep. God does not ask us to deny such pain, but He does give us the provision to overcome it. This book is a testimony of that provision. It contains letters from me to both my wife and my two sons, but they are also letters to myself. They are letters filled with personal, and hopefully worthy, observations of what love deepened in pain is like.

I pledge my wife to heaven for the gospel.
Though our love
each passing day just seems to grow
as I told her when we wed, I would rather
be found dead than love her more than
the one who saved my soul.[2] *- Keith Green*

---

[2] Keith Green, *Pledge My Head to Heaven* (Brentwood, Tenn.: Sparrow Co., 1987).

Chapter 1
Not the Trip We'd Planned!

My Dear Elaine,

    The enclosed letters were written during the long hours of waiting for you to recover from the operation to remove a brain tumor. You came through miraculously but left the hospital unable to communicate at all. You had lost all ability to associate words with objects or to know what objects were for. I remember so often coming into the kitchen and catching you using a spoon for a knife or trying to cut food with the wrong side of a knife. Another time, I walked into the bathroom not surprised to see you combing your hair with a cassette tape.

    I now know that you have no memory of the events that led to your operation or the two months that you spent in the hospital. You often tell the story of not knowing me or the children. In fact, you did not understand why a "doctor" kept visiting you day after day and why he persistently leaned over to kiss you after each visit. It would take months for you to realize that this "doctor" was extremely devoted to you. That person was not the doctor at all but *me*, your husband.

Apparently, you fell in love with me all over again. In your confusion, you began to make plans. When you came out of the hospital, you planned to marry the "doctor." You were also concerned that the three children who kept visiting you did not have parents. You even had a solution to this problem. You and the "doctor" would adopt the three children. I was pleased to see that you were willing, after sixteen years of marriage, to fall in love with me all over again.

Following is what I wrote in my journal during those early weeks of your trial. The journal begins with the trip that we took to the Black Forest in Germany. We had planned that trip meticulously for months following six years of ministry in England. It was to be our last hurrah before returning to America for our first home assignment. We would visit Black Forest Academy (BFA) with the hope of sending Travis there when we returned to England. However, nothing went the way we had planned. Unbeknown to us, that first night in Germany would be the beginning of a bad dream that shortly thereafter turned into a terrible nightmare.

Your best friend,
Mitch

May 29 - June 5, 1998: Germany to Paris

My Dear Elaine,

Your problems began the Friday night that we arrived at the guest house at BFA. You went to bed with a severe headache that by Saturday morning had intensified so much that you spent the whole day in bed. By Sunday morning, I became so concerned that I had a doctor come to see you. After several observations, she concluded that you were suffering from an abscessed tooth. With this assumption, and with a good dose of antibiotics, we decided to move on, as planned, to Paris to visit some good friends who were serving there as missionaries.

Having driven six hours from Germany on Sunday, May 31, we settled down at our friends' house with hopes that the antibiotics would reduce the head pressure. Another doctor examined you on Monday, June 1. He increased the medication and gave you painkillers. By Tuesday, however, you were not any better. You would sit in one spot, wear sunglasses, and stare or sleep. I took the three children to Euro Disney, where we struggled to enjoy ourselves without you. You had planned this trip with scrupulous detail, even arranging for our friends from England, the Dales, to surprise our children at the entrance of Disney.

On Wednesday, another doctor came and looked in your mouth and confirmed that you had an abscess. Looking back, this problem seems so trite. By Wednesday, you were in excruciating pain, especially behind your left eye. You also began to speak irrationally. Perhaps because of the tension and emotional buildup, Joanna, with whom we were staying, and I could not help but laugh at the things you said. It was strange to me to think that an abscessed tooth was causing this behavior, but the doctor assured us that the morphine you were taking might be so strong that this is what caused the disorientation.

On Thursday, you showered and dressed yourself and commented that you felt better. At one point, you took the medicine and said, "Oh, I feel good." You said that a lot, but you didn't say much else. We left our friends at about 2:30, and your last words to them were, "You're wacko to come all time." It made no sense, but I think what you meant was, "You're welcome to come (visit) anytime." They planned to visit in July.

It took three hours to reach Belgium where my parents were, and you slept the whole way. Shortly after we arrived, Dad told us that we should plan on leaving Friday for our home in England to take you to the doctor. I told you this and expected you to resist. Instead, you said "Okay" in a calm, sing-songy voice.

I picked up my younger sister, Viviane, at the Brussels airport with my Mom and Breanna [our daughter] and arrived back about 11:00. Viviane had traveled from Malaysia to visit our grandmother in Belgium, whom she had not seen in years. Our plan was to leave for

Surviving the Fires of Sorrow

England about 1:00 P.M. We had a big lunch, prayed together, packed the car, and said good-bye.

It was a very tearful goodbye, one of the saddest I have ever experienced. Maman Debo [my grandmother] wept and clasped me, and Viviane took it very hard. I did not realize that this would be the last time we would see Maman Debo. (She died while you were in the hospital.) You turned to Viviane and said clearly, "I am really sorry, Viviane," but then you asked for "white rain." I didn't know what you meant by that. The children heard it, too, and we talked about it often. They were aware you were not well. I also knew by this time that you had something much more serious than an abscessed tooth.

I was torn. I wondered whether it would be a risk to drive the long trip to our home in Warrington [northwest England], but in the end, the fact that you would be home won out. We left by 1:30.

Your best friend,
Mitch

Chapter 2
A Pledge for Life!

Day 1: Friday, June 5: Belgium to England

My Dear Elaine,

Our trip home was long. We arrived at Calais at 4:00 and managed to get the 4:09 across the channel to Dover. You needed the bathroom, and when I assisted you, you were not walking straight. I realized that your eyesight was severely affected. I was worried when we arrived at Dover that our trip through London would take us into the heavy Friday afternoon traffic. Amazingly, it flowed, and by 5:00, we were past London.

You were not responding much. I asked you if you were OK, and you merely nodded your head. Near Birmingham, you had to use the bathroom again. I supported you into the BP station where, in the middle of the shop, you stumbled, and your legs gave way under you. I practically had to carry you to the toilet. My head was spinning as though I were in the middle of a bad dream. I picked you up from the floor as about twenty people stood by watching. They no doubt thought that you were drunk or on drugs. I had no interest in explaining to them. By this time, I was confused and scared. I could make no sense of what was happening to you.

Amazingly, we got through Birmingham without heavy traffic to slow us down and arrived at our house at 8:30. It had taken us an unusual eight hours to go from the middle of Belgium to Northern England on a Friday afternoon. Normally, it would have been an eleven-hour trip.

Again, I had to carry you into the house, where you immediately collapsed on the floor. I called our friend Mike who phoned for an ambulance. The children did not seem too concerned and were only a bit excited about the ambulance coming on their turf. They played with their friends, whom they had not seen in two weeks, on the mound just outside our house.

The ambulance arrived at 8:45, and by 9:00, you were at the emergency room. I held back any response to the comment of the ambulance worker that it looked as though you were suffering from exhaustion. If only he knew what our week had been like!

They wheeled you into the emergency room and, after five minutes, placed you in a cubicle. I knew that you were thirsty, but putting you on an IV or giving you water didn't seem to be high on their list of priorities. The first course of action was the gathering of details. It seemed to take them forever. I think that I told five different people what happened. Slowly, they began to realize that your condition was more than exhaustion or an abscessed tooth.

The doctor came, looked at your pupils, checked your reflexes, and finally took a blood sample. The tests showed that you had an infection. Any time I came close to your face to whisper something to you, you smiled. A few times, you moved your lips to kiss me.

At this point, you were not at all familiar with your surroundings. The doctor, armed with the information about an infection, began to check for signs of meningitis. After several hours (I think it was 1:30 in the morning by then), the senior consultant came to inform me that they would have to conduct a brain scan. To do so, they had to place you under general anesthesia. As the team gathered around you to take you for the procedure, they asked me to see you first. I leaned over and kissed you, and then I asked the anesthesiologist if I could pray. They asked if I wanted them to leave, and I said, "No."

I prayed, committing you to our Lord Jesus and asking for your protection. As I left, I turned to them and said, "That prayer was for all of you, too." I left the room caught in a whirlpool of loneliness like I have never known in my life. I stepped outside and wept uncontrollably, only to look up and see an ambulance backing toward me. Until that moment, I didn't realize that I was standing at the entrance of the "Casualty" door where emergency room patients are rushed in.

I realized that I could not go through this trial alone, so at 2:00 I phoned our associate pastor, Andrew Bird, and asked if he would join me. He ended up spending twelve hours with me. A half hour after Andrew arrived, the doctor asked to meet with me. He informed me that the scan had revealed a large mass on your brain. Word was sent to Walton Hospital, a neurological center in Liverpool, along with a copy of the scan. By 5:00, you were in an ambulance racing to Liverpool. I went with Andrew, who beat the speed record while even ignoring red lights. I cannot understand why it took them eight hours to consider your situation an emergency.

At Walton, they scanned you again and prepared you for surgery. One of the surgeons took me aside. His words still echo in my mind.

"You probably know," he said, "that Elaine is very ill. I have to be honest with you. I don't know if she will make it through surgery."

He also explained that it looked as though you had an abscess on the brain, probably caused by a tooth abscess. Another doctor later told me that your pupils were completely fixed, suggesting that your brain was very swollen and under tremendous pressure. That doctor also told me that if we had waited another hour, you would have died.

Andrew and I stayed for four hours. At 10:30, the doctor finally came.

Surviving the Fires of Sorrow

"I thought we were looking for an abscess, but I was shocked to find a tumor the size of a golf ball on her brain, just behind her left eye."

That explained the dizziness, the headaches, and the slurred speech. A lot of things now made sense. You remember, of course, that for a whole year you had complained to our family doctor of dizziness and fainting spells. He had suggested a different diet and adjustments to your birth-control pills, never thinking of recommending a scan. In America, the approach might have been different, and your tumor might have been detected long before it was.

The doctor was confident that the tumor was benign, and he was able to remove the entire growth. I was relieved. During the surgery, as early as 6:00, we had what seemed like the whole world praying for you. I understand that within hours perhaps hundreds of people were already taking your case before the throne of God. Only an hour after the doctor's announcement to me, I was able to visit you.

I loved you so much as you lay there helpless. I determined that I would love you and care for you regardless of what happened. It was not a hard decision to make. I remembered the times when we had expressed our love for each other despite what tragedies might come our way. At the worst point of the experience at Warrington General Hospital, I made the following commitment to God: "Lord, whatever it is that you are asking me to undergo, I tell you now that I am *willing* to accept it." I said it to anchor myself in something solid for those moments when my emotions would overwhelm me. Thus far, I have thrown out many anchors, and they have hit solid ground each time.

Through this time, I have known an unusual peace that I know comes from God. It has not taken away the pain, but it has carried me like a piece of wood is carried by the turbulent waves as they rush toward the shore.

Your best friend

How Elaine and I Fell in Love

Elaine and I were married on July 23, 1983. We were deeply in love. Getting Elaine to fall in love with me, however, did not come without some cost. You could say that our pledge was born of tragedy.

One day during summer vacation, I received a frantic phone call from Elaine, who was then living in Indiana with her family. I was in Georgia. Her brother Jonathan, eight years older than Elaine, had just fallen from a third-story factory building after a scaffold that he was adjusting collapsed. He landed on a narrow patch of grass, missing the pavement by several feet. The impact of the fall was enough, however, to crush his ribs, puncture his lung, and cause multiple breaks in his legs. He was in the hospital, his life hanging by a thread.

"Will you come to see me?" she asked.

At this point, our relationship had grown cold, and I honestly did not see much hope for it. This tragedy and my involvement in it, however, brought us together again and sealed our love.

When I saw Jonathan, it did not seem that he would live. He was conscious and able to speak some, but the injuries to his lungs were extensive. Several days later, his situation was compounded by a stroke caused by a blood clot that had traveled from his injured leg to his brain. Jonathan would recover from his injuries, but he would suffer permanently from the stroke. It would take years for him to regain his speech and reading and writing abilities, a battle that Elaine herself is fighting even as I write this.

Several years after Jonathan's accident, Elaine and I discussed what we would do if the other faced an injury like Jonathan's. Each time the discussion came up, we took the opportunity to pledge that we would do all that we could to demonstrate selfless love and unfailing commitment. Now, I was revisiting that commitment to Elaine in the confines of her hospital room.

Chapter 3
A Revisit to Childhood Pain!

Day 2: Saturday, June 6: Walton Hospital, Liverpool

My Dear Elaine,

    Saturday is a blur in my mind. After your surgery, I made many phone calls to let people know about the situation and to get as much prayer support as possible. At 1:00 P.M., Andrew took me home where some good friends were watching the children. I told the children what had happened, and we all kissed and cried. Especially Breanna, then eight years old, held me and repeated over and over, "Daddy, I love you."

    Things seemed normal at home, but not for long. Two wonderful ladies from the church took all of our vacation clothes and washed them. The house was clean, and many people called. My mother came that night, but I did not wait for her to arrive before going to the hospital. A friend picked her up, and his wife stayed with the children while I left to see you. The trip to the hospital took half an hour each way.

Finally at your bedside, I held your hand and rubbed your arms, feet, and legs. It was so good just to be with you and to see you alive. Yet, in many ways you did not look yourself. Your body looked artificial, bloated like a blown-up doll. But I knew that beneath the swelling, you were desperately fighting for your life. No one could tell me what would happen. Survival rested completely in the hands of our Lord. What could I do but lean over you and commit you to Jesus? And that I would do repeatedly.

I had arranged to sleep in a flat [apartment] belonging to the hospital, but when I arrived at 10:30, it was so dirty that I got only as far as the sheets. I needed to be in my own home with my family. I called Mom and told her that I was coming home. By 11:30, I was fast asleep in our own bed. The sheets were clean.

I slept soundly and awoke about the same time that Travis did. He hopped in bed with me, and we held each other closely. He's handled it well and has not seemed to internalize it all that much. Breanna has been more emotional but usually only when she sees me cry. Brett (four years old) is not fully aware of things. He acts just like his normal self.

Your best friend

Day 3: Sunday, June 7

My Dear Elaine,

I gathered the children together about 9:00 A.M. and read to them the story of Jesus' healing of Peter's mother from Mark's Gospel. You and I have been reading from Mark at night, so I thought that this passage would be appropriate. The love and compassion of our Lord Jesus toward those who suffer is so rich to me right now. For the first time in my life, I understand what it truly means to hurt for someone else. The pain I experienced as a child in suffering from depression was my own, but now my pain is completely for you. I am experiencing a true heart of love, a new depth of empathy. I have thought a lot about my childhood sickness since you have been sick. I can't seem to shake it. Perhaps God is showing me that He was using my experience to prepare me for this and to be strong for you.

Your best friend

My Story

When I was twelve, I wanted to die because living no longer seemed possible. Later, I discovered that the cause of this depression was a chemical imbalance created by the usual biological changes that normally occur in a preteen boy. However, I suspect that the reasons were more complex than that.

The changes in my life to that point *had* been complex and many. I grew up in the home of missionary parents who left Europe in 1957 to begin thirty-eight years of ministry to the stone-age people of Irian Jaya, Indonesia (now Papua). I was born in a village high in the mountains at the Wissel Lakes. When I reached six, there were no local schools for me to attend, so I was sent to boarding school. My older brother and sister were already there, and I had been prepared to accept this arrangement as the normal thing to do.

However, from that first moment when I sat in the little single-engine airplane and waved through the small, foggy window at my parents, something in me cried out that this was *not* natural. I remember vividly being given a small gift that I was not to open until the plane was well out of the sight of our mission station. It was a small consolation for what would become a pattern of reunions and separations for the next twelve years of my life. I fared well and even considered these early years to be happy and productive.

But at twelve years of age, all of that changed. The crisis began in my second semester of sixth grade. After two weeks, the usual homesick feelings did not wear off as they had earlier. Homesickness gave way to a growing sense of despair. I would wake up in the morning crying for no reason. I was confused, sad, and increasingly desperate. Teachers and dorm parents did not know how to respond. To them, my behavior seemed like normal childhood rebellion.

After a month, word reached my parents that my state was becoming increasingly uncontrollable, so the school made plans for them to visit. By this time, I was desperate. One night, I threatened to run away, and I did. One of the teachers heard that I had left my room and began to look for me along the trail that led from the school compound. I can remember seeing him pass me as I hid in a ditch about a quarter of a mile from the school. About an hour later, I decided to go back to my room. I cried for hours in my bed. The only comfort I received the next morning from this teacher was a scolding and a slap on the face.

My mom came, and I found relief by her presence. However, that relief was short-lived, so I cried for my father. My situation only worsened, forcing my parents to remove me from school.

I did alright for several weeks at home, but then that unexplainable sense of despair returned. It is most vivid to my memory when I recall a boat trip that I took with my father to an outpost station. Looking back on it now, I see the experience in that boat symbolizing the turmoil that had sucked all hope and joy from my being. The lake was calm and the winds were light, but in my mind I did not see it that way. Despite the water being smooth on every side and the waves only tossing lightly against the boat, I cried in fear.

"We are going to die!" I screamed. My father reassured me that we would not, but my cry went beyond any fear for our physical safety. It was my soul that was in torment. I had been drawn into an unseen turmoil, and the demons of that storm whipped at me from every side. I was helpless.

This experience and the general deterioration of my condition led my parents to consult a missionary physician, who recommended that I be sent to Australia for treatment. I spent three months with my father in Sydney, where I began undergoing psychiatric evaluation. I first grasped the seriousness of the situation when my father informed me one day that we would move into our own place. Up until then, we had been guests in the house of an Australian family. I felt some excitement over this, but that excitement was shattered when I read the sign welcoming us to that new "home." It said something about a psychiatric treatment center.

Some messed-up people were in that house, and in my view, I was the only normal one there. I might have been normal, but I was also seriously ill. We were later informed that without the extensive treatment that I received during the following years, I could have turned out very badly indeed. At a follow-up visit the next year, one psychiatrist told my father that I likely would never finish high school, let alone make it as far as college.

It would take three years before I was weaned from the medication that, with the help of good psychiatric care, brought about a healthy equilibrium to my life. I know that this experience and God's intervention at that time are the very things that give me strength today.

Treatments aside, the greatest medicine to my recovery was the love of my parents. When we were released to return home, I spent the next two years with them. They then decided that I would be better off with continued professional help that was not available in the village. The best option offered to us was to move to the United States, a completely foreign country to me and my family. So we moved to Atlanta, Georgia, where I received further help from a Christian psychiatrist for two more years. Today I am overwhelmed that my parents chose so easily to suspend their career as missionaries for my well-being. Being missionaries was their life, and they completely accepted that when they left Papua with me, they might be saying good-bye to their adopted country for the last time.

I am not sure what, if any, bearing my early boarding-school experience had on my sickness, but I do not have an ounce of bitterness toward my parents. They did the best they could with what was available. What bitterness I could have had was absorbed completely by their deep love for me and their willingness to give up everything to ensure that I received the best care. Later, you will read how this sacrifice had uncanny similarities to my own relationship with my oldest son and years later with my youngest son. Both boys were twelve when diagnosed with cancer, the same age as me when I was diagnosed with depression. More on that later.

Thanks to my childhood crisis, my view of God was shaped in the construction room of pain. In my confined anguish, my only hope was God. One solitary strand held my life, and it was the thread that secured me to God. Take the story of Jonah in the Bible. Jonah's last thread, when all others were cut, was the one that mattered. There in the belly of the fish, literally at the bottom of the ocean, Jonah had his best and really his first view of God. In that hell Jonah met God, and he declared, "In my *distress* I called to the LORD, and he answered me. From the *depths of the grave* I called for help, and you listened to my cry.... I have been *banished* from your sight; yet I will look again toward your holy temple.... [T]o the roots of the mountains I *sank* down; the *earth beneath barred me* in forever. But you brought my life up from the pit, O LORD my God" (Jonah 2:2, 4, 6, emphasis added).

*****

My Dear Elaine,

It is still Sunday, and this is my second letter to you today. Your good friend Jeanette picked the children up at 9:30 for Sunday school, and Mom and I drove to Liverpool to see you. Brett was all excited about church, because he would be going with the *big children* during church time. Mom was such a support on this visit. In the waiting room, she read to me portions of Psalm 34, which strengthened us both. "The righteous cry out, and the Lord hears them; he delivers them from all their troubles. The Lord is close to the brokenhearted and saves those who are crushed in spirit" (Ps. 34: 17, 18).

Several families here at the neurological center are "crushed in spirit," and I have asked them to read this passage. Most of the people here are in crisis. Everyone in the waiting room is facing the tragedy of a loved one near death. Some of them have head injuries. One lady waits to hear how her husband will fare following a sudden collapse caused by a brain aneurysm. I remember Charles Spurgeon writing that this world is like a hospital ward; everywhere people are hurting or dying. Death and sickness are everywhere. Well, this hospital waiting room is a microcosm of the world. This is the real world. Everything "out there" is an illusion.

Your vital signs have been good. I've learned a lot about watching monitors and what changes in numbers reflect about the body. One number especially is important – the one that indicates the pressure on your brain. When the number is too high, it means there is too much pressure, perhaps caused by further bleeding. Checking your pupils regularly is also important. The right eye is responding well to the light of the flashlight, but the left eye continues to be sluggish, and the pupil is bigger than the right one. The nurses place numbers and letters on a large chart to mark your progress. At the end of the day, a doctor reviews the chart to see the progress on blood pressure, brain pressure, heart-beat, pupil size, etc.

The nurses have been professional. Here in the ICU, there is one nurse per patient, and your nurses are top class. When I have a question, they immediately stop what they are doing and respond patiently. Two other patients, Peter and Jane, have been in the room. Both of them have had a brain injury of some sort.

Today Nick, my friend and pastor at the United Reform Church, visited, and in the evening I brought the children to see you. It is good that I did, because they need to know where you are and what your true condition is. Otherwise, they might create a fantasy in their minds. At first, they seemed hesitant, but the nurse explained the tubes, needles, and charts to them, and they finally relaxed. Jeanette also came and, after seeing you, took the children home. I stayed until about 9:45, then I went to bed relaxed and encouraged. All of your vital signs are good, and I am hopeful that they will try to wake you on Monday morning.

Chapter 4
Painful Lessons!

Day 4: Monday, June 8

My Dear Elaine,

At 12:30 A.M., the phone rang. I thought that it must be your parents because they had not phoned on Sunday, but it was the nurse. Your brain pressure was increasing to a dangerous level, so they needed to do another scan. She told me not to come until the scan results were back. Amazingly, I fell back asleep without worrying. At this point, we had no idea whether you would live or die. I was prepared for death.

About one hour later, the nurse called again, and to my relief the scan did not show any bleeding or clotting. I slept well again.

The consultants met, reviewed your situation, and decided that it was probably not wise to wake you yet. They might try to do so tomorrow. I hope so. To me, waking you will be a determining moment. Will you come out of it, or will you remain in a coma? Will you have extensive brain damage, or will you look up at me and chat away as though nothing has happened? Might you be a vegetable for the rest of your life? My mind virtually replayed pictures of Nancy, your brother's sister-in-law, every time I thought of that prospect.

Thirty years ago, Nancy was in a car accident and sustained serious brain damage. Since then, she has remained completely immobile in a back room at her parent's house. When one looks at Nancy, there is no way of determining whether she knows herself or is aware of her situation. Her eyes move, and she makes sounds, but that is it. Perhaps she has been completely cognizant of life around her but is trapped in her body and has been unable to give any hints of her inner awareness.

The consultant assigned to you met with us about an hour later. His name is Dr. Miles, and he has a reputation for being brutally blunt. After speaking to him, I felt defeated. Because of the heavy swelling just before surgery, a good possibility exists of extensive brain damage. Perhaps he wants to keep my expectations in check. I don't know! I've been here all day, and I plan to spend the night. Mom thought that Dad should come from Belgium, so she has called him, and he is looking into flights possibly for this week. My sister Viviane will probably go home to Malaysia. She has no reason to stay.

My good friend John Rockley came tonight and surprised me by bringing Breanna. Oh, how good it was to see her. It made my day! They also brought food. We went for a walk, and with Breanna there, of course we had to play tag. It was good to get out. I had not been outside the building since noon. John stayed for a while, and I enjoyed my tea (supper). It was good to hold Breanna. Travis was not up to coming, and Brett cried when he couldn't come.

I just visited you again, and you are doing well. Your vital signs have been stable all day. When I'm in here with you, I usually stay from forty-five minutes to an hour. I rub your arms, legs, and feet. I talk to you, and one time, when no one was looking, I sang to you. Hopefully you weren't able to hear that. It was *horriiiible*, as Brett would say.

I called Mom, and many people have been calling her. Several of them let me know that they are fasting for you. Even Sami Dagher called to say that his church in Beirut, Lebanon would take time to fast and pray.

(Sami, well known for his work in restoring spiritual life to Lebanon following the war, was with us in Warrington just two weeks before Elaine fell ill. Sami really took to Elaine because of her desire to help him find a pair of shoes for his British mother-in-law, who lived with them in Beirut. Sami had brought one shoe with him to find a match that would please his mother-in-law. Elaine spent several hours going from store to store looking for those shoes. And yes, she did find them. Sami would later call several times a week, referring to Elaine as England's true queen.)

The love from people worldwide has been overwhelming. I can do nothing to repay them, but I realize that no one is asking that of me. I hope that tomorrow you will wake up. If not, I accept that. I am willing to love you forever. I will care for you, nurture you, and protect you — not because I have to but because I want to.

Your best friend

Day 5: Tuesday, June 9

My Dear Elaine,

I came early today because there was a good chance that they would wake you. This expectation has become an obsession with me. I think about nothing else. We can know nothing of your condition until you awake.

I left the house at 7:00 and arrived at the hospital by 8:00. They immediately told me that they would scan you, and if all looked good, they would wake you up. Mom arrived about 8:45 with my friend Dass, a church deacon. At 9:00, they took you in for the scan. While you were there, Larry Carey, our mission field director, came. He stayed with us about four hours. At 9:30, they wheeled you back through the poorly working elevators which seem to take five minutes to open. I don't know what the medical staff does in an emergency. When you returned, the doctor gave me a thumbs up. The swelling in your brain had gone down. They would wake you.

Within an hour, the doctor simply had to hit a switch to cut the flow of the drug that made you comatose, and it was now a matter of waiting. First, your head moved slightly, then your left arm, and then your right arm and leg. It was a relief to see the right side move, because the doctors were concerned that pressure on the left side of the brain might affect the right side of the body. During that time, your sister Kathleen called and was reassured to hear that you were stirring. Then you said your first words to me.

"Come on, man," you said. (I think you said that because you were frustrated by all of the tubes and wires on your body.) These would be some of the only clear words you would utter for months. You couldn't stand the ventilator in your mouth. I spent hours wrestling your left arm to keep you from grabbing at the tubes. You also kept grabbing at the bandage on your head. The nurses liked when I was there because I was doing their work for them. Diane is the best nurse. She reminds me a lot of you.

Because you were so wiggly, they injected you with morphine. You have been very uncomfortable. Another patient, Steven, has been assigned to your room and is in the bed next to you. He's from Warrington and fell down some stairs drunk, I'm told. He had serious bleeding in his brain. People are at this hospital only because they suffer. I would later harbor a lot of anger toward Steven, not because of anything that happened between us but simply because his situation showed me how unfair life is.

Steven had been partying late with his friends, and his fall down the stairs came about when he arrived home. He literally cracked his head open, and the doctors were certain that he would not live. I felt for him but more for his family. Yet, inwardly I fought the feeling that Steven was getting what he deserved. He probably did not know the Lord Jesus, so he would sadly live for eternity separated from God. Steven would certainly die. The doctors thought so, and so did I.

Two weeks later, I entered the hospital to see you and almost fainted as I passed a man speaking on the phone. It was Steven. I tried very hard to be excited for him, but I could not. Here you were in terrible shape because of a brain tumor, certainly no fault of your own. But he was drunk, irresponsible, and stupid. And while he was speaking on the phone, fully recovered, you were still fighting for your life.

I am told that at home the phone is ringing off the hook. Among the calls is one from our regional director, John Harvey. I have received nearly forty e-mails and plan on printing them. The church held a prayer meeting tonight, as they have each night. Tonight, so many people were at the associate pastor's house that some of them had to sit on the stairs. Your brother, Jonathan, left a message and hopes to speak to me soon. I went to bed much more relaxed and confident. God has been so good and so have His people. I called the ward before going to bed to be sure that you were okay!

Your best friend

Ministry and Pain

Elaine and I learned early in our ministry that you cannot separate ministry from your personal life. Neither can you separate ministry from suffering. We have a hard time with that fact, particularly those of us who come from the Western world.

No one has taught me more about the relationship between suffering and ministry than the prophet Jeremiah. His desire to serve God, like mine, needed to go through the fires of sorrow.

Life seemed unfair to Jeremiah. A willing and available servant of the Lord should not have to suffer thus. If a protective shield existed for God's servants, his seemed to have the cracks of a worn vessel. Told to go to the potter's house (Jer. 18:1-6), Jeremiah took the lesson from God and began to preach it fervently. The message involved God's desire and need to place Israel on the potter's wheel to shape something new from her marred condition. God would do what seemed best to Him, but only when Israel was like clay in His hands.

Jeremiah was not well received. People did not like his message and neither did they like Jeremiah. Jeremiah faithfully preached God's word exactly as he was told, and he suffered for it. (See Jeremiah 20:1-2 for the extent of that suffering.) It did not take long for Jeremiah to question the justice of his situation. He took his case to the Lord.

"O Lord, you deceived me, and I was deceived; … I am ridiculed all day long; everyone mocks me…. So the word of the Lord has brought me insult and reproach all day long" (Jer. 20:7-8).

Do you hear Jeremiah's cry? "Lord, I have done everything you have asked me to do. I have been faithful and godly, and this is my reward for all of that?"

It didn't make sense to Jeremiah that rebuke and scorn should be the reward for faithful service. "Come on, God!" he must have cried. "Is this what happens to those of us who willingly place ourselves in your hands? Lord, I have given my life to serve you. Is this the reward? Lord, I want to serve you, but does it have to hurt?"

Jeremiah's pain, however, became a breeding ground for passion. His suffering became the context for a renewed longing to serve. Pressed and pressured from every side, broken and hurt, Jeremiah discovered how much God really meant to him. Note what he believed and expressed: "But if I say, 'I will not mention him or speak anymore in his name,' his word is like a fire, a fire shut up in my bones. I am weary of holding it in; indeed, I cannot" (Jer. 20:9).

From the very beginning of Elaine's trial, I became aware that this was an experience of life that God was using to renew my love for Him. Looking back, I realize that God also had been using some other trials to achieve this goal in my life, but I was not as good of a student back then. It is fascinating that our missionary work began in suffering, and this first term was ending in suffering. We were only six weeks away from our first home assignment when Elaine fell ill.

In July 1992, we were only two weeks away from moving to England to begin our missionary career. One morning, Elaine woke up feeling feverish. It was a hot summer day, and while the children splashed water on each other in their grandparents' backyard, Elaine slept through most of that day. The next morning, her situation worsened. Her glands were swollen; she was sore all over. She slept on. Several days passed with no improvement, so we decided to take her to the doctor. I had heard of mononucleosis but never knew how debilitating it could be. Tests confirmed that Elaine had it.

In my ignorance, I chose to delay our departure by only two weeks. I really thought that I was doing Elaine a big favor. We did not feel very triumphant about what should have been an exciting new venture. In the airplane, Elaine groaned and complained of pain, and she was extremely tired.

Oh well, I thought, *in several days she will perk up and begin to conquer this new frontier with me.* It would take her three months before she even began to feel well. I feel sorry now that during those months I dragged her with me to sightsee in the countryside and break new ground in our ministry.

Elaine would later see this sickness as a blessing. God would use her suffering to make a soft entry in a society where Americans have a tendency to be loud and overbearing. Having just moved from Texas, where volume is an asset, the risk of offending our new friends was high. Usually outgoing and energetic, Elaine spent her first three months in England unusually quiet and reserved, undoubtedly a British asset. She now thanks God for that fact. She often recounts how, when she visited people, all of the energy she could muster was to nod her head and say, "Yes, yes."

Elaine did not often keep a journal, but I discovered that she used up a good bit of ink sorting through her emotions during this trial with mononucleosis (glandular fever). She has given me her permission to include some of those thoughts here. She wrote the following on July 26, 1992:

> As I struggle in my weakness against this mono, I am reading of King David. It comes to mind that surely he did not particularly

enjoy being chased in the caves and wilderness and having his life threatened. Not exactly the thing to plan for a summer's holiday. And my sickness is not <u>at all</u> what I would plan for my first months in England. So, I have to seek the Lord. The alternative is to complain. It seems a strange thing that I would be sick at a time like this. But, it was also strange that David, the future King of Israel, the anointed of God, the chosen one, would be fleeing for his life.

I often reflected on this entry years later while Elaine was fighting for her life. I wondered what God would do through this more serious trial. All that I knew to do was to place the situation in the hands of the Potter. He would know what to do with it.

Chapter 5
Where Is God in All of This?

(A Struggle with God's Sovereignty)

Elaine now carefully speculates how different things would be for her had I made different decisions when she fell ill. I fight off guilt and try hard not to lay too much responsibility on my shoulders for my ignorance and poor judgment. Looking back, of course, I would have done things differently. I also realize that had the tumor been detected earlier that week and operated on in an elective manner, Elaine's situation would be different now. She would not have suffered as severely as she did.

As it was, her surgery to remove the tumor was performed to save her life. The surgeons quickly removed not only the tumor, but also a portion of her brain. We really had no time to consider what effect this sort of aggressive surgery would have on Elaine. What her condition would be if she lived was a secondary consideration at the time.

Because the tumor was located on the speech center, the consequence to this life-saving measure was severe. With an elective surgery, the surgeon talks to the patient and discusses the risks. In this case, however, there was no time for such an option. The response was severe and urgent.

Since the summer of 1998, I have spent more time pondering who God is than I ever did before. Before, my understanding of God was so "pat." He was definable and easily explained. I even preached some good sermons on the sovereignty of God. I had fallen into the trap of assuming that I understood Him. Such is no longer the case.

If you want an honest conversation about the sovereignty of God, don't go to a Bible college professor, although his knowledge and training should equip him with all of the right theological explanations. I would suggest, instead, that you sit in the waiting room of a hospital where some family members await the results of life-saving surgery. Speak to someone who is hurting, and then you will appreciate the real struggles of trying to understand God.

All of this brings me to agonize over the whole issue of God's sovereignty in relationship to the choices that each of us makes in life. I say this with the realization that several simple decisions could have radically changed the course of events. For example, several weeks before our family left for our vacation in Germany, I received a phone call from our regional director asking if I would be available to take a vision trip to Bosnia for our mission. I explained that, although I was eager to take the trip, I thought canceling our plans for Germany would be impractical. Now we recognize that had I gone, Elaine would have been at home in England where our family doctor might have pursued a more aggressive course of action based on her symptoms.

I am also haunted by the decisions that I made to continue our planned trip from Germany to Paris and then to Belgium rather than admit her to a local hospital. How different would things have been? What would have happened if the doctors who saw Elaine both in Germany and Paris had insisted that she be admitted to the hospital right away? What is the relationship of God's sovereignty to our choices and actions? What should our response as Christians be when things would have turned out better for us if we had only made different decisions or choices?

I believe firmly in God's sovereignty, but I also believe in the free will of man, at least as free as we can be in the bounded reality of sin. I believe that God gives us space to move and room to make decisions—even to make mistakes. I cannot articulate how a sovereign God remains sovereign over everything even when we mess things up. But what I do know is this: as a sovereign God, He takes all of what we go through and shapes it to form what He wants. I also know that I can take the guilt, the "what ifs," and the agony and tell God all about them. That is the wonder of serving a sovereign God. He can take the messed-up situations, sometimes even those problems that we ourselves create, and redeem them for His own glory. "For from him and through him and to him are all things. To him be the glory forever! Amen" (Rom. 11:36 NIV).

My conviction of God's sovereignty permits me to live with the unanswered questions and, yes, the mystery as well. I can believe that God is sovereign without having to explain how that makes sense in light of human experience. God is in control. That truth is sufficient for me. I can walk away from an unexplained event and simply live with an assurance that somehow He manages it all for our good and for His glory. Oswald Chambers summarized it well when he said: "God does not tell us what He is going to do; He reveals who He is."[3]

I recently read Gerald Sittser's book *A Grace Disguised*. It is an attempt to make some sense of the tragic car accident that claimed the lives of his mother, his wife, and his daughter. As a theology professor who admits to thinking that he knew God, Sittser faced the overwhelming realization that he really did not know God. He wrote the following about the sovereignty of God:

---

[3] Chambers, *My Utmost for His Highest*, Jan. 2.

Prior to the accident, I held a narrow view of his sovereignty, though I did not realize it at the time. I was inclined to believe that God simply pulled the strings and manipulated the events of our lives as if we were marionettes on a string and God was a puppeteer controlling us completely. I believe now that my view of God's sovereignty was far too small. His sovereignty encompasses all of life—for example, not simply tragic experiences but also our responses to them. It envelops all of human experiences and integrates it into a greater whole. Even human freedom, then, becomes a dimension of God's sovereignty, as if God were a novelist who had invented characters so real that the decisions they make are genuinely their decisions.[4]

To believe that God is sovereign does not require that I comprehend all that this doctrine entails. Our suffering presents us with a more awesome and far more mysterious God than the convenient, predictable Creator we assume in our time of peace. But if suffering presents us with the true God, are we not forced to see that our pain has tremendous value to offer those who suffer? I am beginning to see that it does.

Suffering peels away our nurtured preconceptions of God, introducing us to God as He truly is. No wonder Job could say during his suffering what he never could have said before: "I know that you can do all things; no plan of yours can be thwarted...Surely I spoke of things I did not understand, things too wonderful for me to know...My ears had heard of you but now my eyes have seen you. Therefore I despise myself and repent in dust and ashes" (Job 42:2-3, 5-6).

---

[4] Gerald Sittser, A Grace Disguised (Grand Rapids: Zondervan, 1995), 141.

Chapter 6
The World as Seen from a Waiting Room

Day 6: Wednesday, June 10

My Dear Elaine,

    I woke at 4:00 and called again. You were fine, sleeping and relaxed in fact. At 7:00, I called my brother JP who was to leave for Australia with his family. He wanted to speak to me before they left. This situation has greatly affected him, as it has my oldest sister Ruthy. When Ruthy called on Sunday, we both wept. Elaine, you're so loved. How good to know that my family loves you so much! Times such as this reveal how much a person like you touches the lives of so many people.

    I took the children to school today to give them a sense of normal routine. It was good to be home with them last night and to put them to bed. Some of the routine and discipline has been lost.

Surviving the Fires of Sorrow

After they were in bed, Mom and I headed over to see you. My heart always beats more quickly when I reach that last traffic light before turning right into Walton Hospital. I rang the bell, and when we were invited in, I saw you looking so much fresher and healthier. You were still drowsy but moving more. Overnight you had told the nurses to "get away." Your words are clear and appropriate to the setting. At one point, I asked you if you were okay, and you said, "Yah." At another time, I asked if I could squeeze your hand, and you said, "OK." Single words have never sounded so good. At least you have not told me to get away.

(These single phrases would be the only clear words that Elaine would say for months. For some reason, when she came to, her words were gibberish. One of the surgeons who assisted in the surgery told me in the hallway that he was confident that the tumor was not on the speech center. His assessment, however, turned out to be wrong. It was later confirmed that the tumor was precisely at the center of Elaine's center of speech. She was in for a battle. Apparently, the few clear statements that she made on those particular days were instinctive and not processed cognitively. The real challenge would come when she tried to express her thoughts. I remember how weeks later, in my ignorance, I sat next to her with pen and paper writing down what she said and trying to decipher the meaning of each sound. I had never heard of fluency aphasia, so I naively assumed that Elaine would very quickly speak normally. I could never have been more wrong.)

The doctors have told me that you will be moved out of the ICU this afternoon to a high-dependency unit (HDU). This is real progress. Karl, the Chinese pastor in Manchester, and his wife Lydia came by, and Karl prayed for you. By his volume, he seemed to be covering the whole ward with his prayers.

Karl and Lydia brought flowers, but there was no room for them in the ward; we took them home instead. At 2:00, they moved you out of the ICU to the other ward. What a joy!

Mom and I were sitting in the waiting room anticipating word of your transfer. Sitting beside us was a middle-aged woman accompanied by her daughter. In such a situation, it is normal to ask about their circumstances. It turns out that her ex-husband is the man who is fighting for his life right next to you, Elaine. He had fallen while working on his house and sustained serious brain injuries. He was dying, and the doctors did not hold out much hope. Well, within several minutes, the dying man's brother entered the room along with the man's current wife. Suddenly, the room was filled with tension.

"What are *you* doing here?" the brother yelled beyond us to the ex-wife, who was beginning to cry. "You have nothing to do with Tom, so leave!"

So much for British reserve.

"You leave him, break his heart, and think that you can just show up like this? Go! Leave! *Now!*"

By this time, the poor woman was sobbing uncontrollably, and her daughter was trying vainly to cover her with her arms. To our knowledge, the situation was never resolved. In fact, the ex-wife tried to enter the ICU and was literally forced away by the brother. I have since concluded that hospitals are not the best place to patch up broken relationships. The truth is that family tragedy can bring to the surface things that previously had been comfortably contained. People manage well with their sins until God reminds them how finite they are.

The conversations in that waiting room were the most honest and real that one could ever have. People who are faced with the death of a loved one can be painfully realistic about life. I prayed daily that God would use me in that waiting room. I tried to ask more questions rather than share my own pain. If pressed, I could tell them that although you were in bad shape, God was in it. He would help. Steering the conversation away from myself to Jesus helped me to deal with it as well. I did not want to become self-absorbed.

Your room upstairs in the new unit is so much better than the ICU. It has more space and is easier for visiting, and it is not as tense as the ICU, where all of the patients are in critical condition. The nurses are kind and seem more relaxed. They will take good care of you. Your nurse today is Claire, and she's really nice. I took Mom home at 4:00, stopping first at the bank and Birchwood Center for some odds and ends. The mall was strangely empty because of the kickoff of the soccer World Cup at 4:30, Scotland versus Brazil. I managed to be home in time to watch it on TV with Travis.

The Dales pick up Breanna and Travis each afternoon, and Brett spends most of his time with the neighbors. The children are all doing well. I take time each day to talk with them. After watching soccer, about 6:30, I came back to Walton with Breanna to see you. You were fast asleep, so we decided to go home after an hour. Breanna was a good nurse, squeezing your hands and speaking to you. She has such a tender way with you. I have grown to love her deeply as I watch her suffer with you.

The children's school has had special times of prayer for you. Many of the cards that you have received are very touching. One card from a friend especially moved me. She wrote, "I was shocked when I heard you were going back to America, but that was nothing compared to this. You must know how much I feel for you and how much I like your warmth, patience, sense of humor and openness. No wonder you are such a wonderful 'mum.' Sometimes when I am in a situation where my patience is tried, I try to think what you might do. Hope you get well soon."

Your best friend

Chapter 7
An Expression of True Commitment

Day 7: Thursday, June 11

My Dear Elaine,

    It's hard to believe that a week has gone by since we drove from Paris to my grandmother's place in Belgium. If we had known then what we know now, we would not have gone.

    I called the ward from home at 7:30 this morning. You are still asleep. The children slept late today, except for Brett who snuggled with me for at least half an hour. The children have been a real source of strength. Travis is now convinced that he is sleeping late because he's nearing the teen years when the body needs more sleep.

    "You only grow when you're asleep, you know," he tells me.

    Breanna asked me if your continuous sleep meant that you would be much fatter. Her grin told me that it was a joke. Jan Meir, one of your good friends, popped by to offer help with rides for the children, but I wanted to take them today. We read Philippians 4:13 together first and prayed. "It is God who is at work in you both to will and act according to his good pleasure." I encouraged the children to think about this verse during the day. I left for the hospital about 8:55, arriving about 9:30.

Since you have moved to the third floor, Sherington Ward, the elevator has cooperated nicely. Before, we would have to wait five minutes for it to reach our floor, and sometimes it just bypassed us.

Alex is working the shift this morning. You stirred very little. I was expecting more today, but I need to be patient. Roger, my Anglican vicar friend, showed up with flowers and stayed about half an hour which was encouraging. He also prayed for you. Jeanette brought Brett, and he sat on the side of your bed and stroked your hand. I sat next to you and spent most of the time reading a Barney book to him. You didn't flinch.

I have been alone with you for several hours, and just a few minutes ago you stirred. For the first time, you opened your eyes wide and smiled at me before falling fast asleep. What a lift! I will sit here and wait patiently for the next time you choose to pop out of your shell. I keep wondering if you're aware of things around you. Will you talk about what this state of unconsciousness is like? Will you remember the last week? What is the last thing you remember? I am beginning to think more of what your first emotions will be when you come to. It will be a relief to us, but what will it be like for you? I imagine that there will be confusion, perhaps even some depression. I will be there to help you. Nothing else matters to me now but you. Time stops in moments of pain. I think very little of the church I pastor at, except about the overwhelming way in which they have reached out to us this past week.

Your best friend

Day 8: Friday, June 12

My Dear Elaine,

Kathleen called last night. I have nothing more to tell her except, "Just wait! Just pray!" I went home around 7:00. I watched a soccer game with Travis and went to bed at 11:00. Travis and I have enjoyed talking at night since we're in the same room. Sometimes I sneak out of bed, find his feet in the sleeping bag, and tickle him. We then wrestle and laugh for several minutes before just holding each other. He is really growing up, but I can sense that he is internalizing his feelings about you.

I woke up early again today. A full week of your life is missing now. The mornings are light, and by 5:30 my body says that it's time to get up. I lie in bed for an hour thinking about very little. I've tried to keep to my disciplines this past week. Devotions have been brief but meaningful. My prayers have mostly centered on you. Today, I thanked God for not only the many people who have helped but also for our friends who do not share our faith. I want so much for God to use this situation to lead them to Himself.

I called the hospital again around 7:00 to get a report on you. You've changed little, they said. I'm getting depressingly used to the typical conversation.

"Hi, I am just calling to see how Elaine is doing."

"Oh, there is really no change. She is still resting."

What else did I expect – that you would jump out of bed and sprint down the hallway?

Your best friend

How I Saw Suffering Open Doors

Ministry has some strange ironies, some of them deeply confounding. We worked for six years with many people who had no interest in God. Although some of them did respond, many of them remained disinterested. Working alongside a gospel-minded church, we were able to capitalize on many creative ways to reach this secular community. Some of our methods were quite innovative, and we simply took the lack of interest as evidence of people's hardness of heart. Certainly, it was not due to our inability to communicate the gospel effectively – or was it?

Here is the twist: it was now in our helplessness and complete dependence on God that we noticed a receptivity in people. For example, one friend made statements about faith and expressed her struggles with God in the presence of our utter weakness. Yet when we had spoken with her earlier, at a time when everyone seemed so healthy, she had seemed to ignore us. Later, when Travis was dying, many people called us from England. They told us things about their own beliefs that they never would have told us when we were there in our official capacity. After Travis died, the community of Birchwood held a memorial service for him, and more than two hundred people attended, half of whom had never attended church.

Several months later, we were returning to our home in northeast Georgia after a busy day of shopping. Our daughter Breanna insisted that she be the one given the duty of opening the front door for us. I gave her the set of keys and watched her fumble with each one until she found one that she thought would fit the keyhole. None of the keys seemed to unlock the door. Frustrated, she handed the keys to me and stepped back. I placed the right key into the keyhole only to discover that the door had never been locked. Breanna was fighting to unlock a door that was already open.

I believe that in our ministry for God we often are like that. We try key after key only to find ourselves frustrated when none of our keys, or methods, seem to open the door to people's hearts. Only in our exasperation do we turn the set of keys over to God, who gently moves us to the side to reveal that the door has been open all along. The door to our ministry in Birchwood was never locked. We try so hard in ministry to get people to change until we realize that God is the only one who can bring about change in them, and the methods He uses to do it often humble us.

Like our suffering. His suffering. Like the cross.

His way had that effect on Jonah. That Old Testament prophet thought that he was indispensable to God. He honestly believed that if he ran from God, God could not do what He had in mind. This spiritual arrogance led Jonah to run from God with a self-confidence reserved only for fools. Through the shock of pain (by allowing Jonah to spend three days in the belly of a fish), God taught Jonah that he was not all that important to God's ability to work. In fact, by the end of his testimony, we find Jonah sulking on the sidelines as he watches God do what He wanted, this time without Jonah's help.

No wonder Jesus pointed to Jonah's own *death* and *resurrection* (his time in the fish) as a foreshadowing to His own death and resurrection (see Matthew 12:40) and *that* becoming our only hope in this life. The only message we have is the cross of Jesus, and it is in our suffering that we can point others to that truth.

I have chosen not to sulk. Rather, I marvel at how God works not only in us, but also *in spite of* us. Serving Him in suffering has been a privilege, and being asked to continue serving Him, when we are now broken and weak, is an honor.

Chapter 8
Ministry at Arm's Length

Day 9: Saturday, June 13

My Dear Elaine,

    Today I almost gave up. I've been so depressed. It seems that you will never wake up. It did not help when I asked the doctor some questions about your prognosis. Due to the tremendous swelling that occurred in your brain before the operation, there is a good chance of brain damage. There is even a chance that you will be in a vegetative state. I left the hospital this morning in tears. I cried out to God on the way home and told Him that I could take it no longer. When I arrived home, I could not hide my emotions from Mom and Dad. Mom wept with me. I have shed many tears this week.

    I returned to see you again around 4:00. You have a lot of drainage from the incision, and the doctors are concerned about an infection. Just as I arrived, they took you for a CAT scan on the ground floor. I went along. It struck me that this is where it began just over a week ago. I could still see myself in the chair, trying to take in what the surgeon was telling me: they had to operate right away, and you might not live through it. Praise God, you are alive! This time, you were too wiggly during the scan, so they asked me to hold your chin for the five minutes that the machine rotated taking pictures of your brain. Later, the scan revealed no swelling or infection.

The afternoon was rather uneventful. I simply sat next to you and looked at your eyes. I think that I did that for hours. Usually, I read or watch soccer, but I couldn't do that then. For the first time, you responded directly to my words. I leaned over and said, "Elaine, your head really hurt last week, didn't it?"

You responded immediately, "It does hurt."

Another glimmer of hope!

Around 6:00, three different friends came. Their visits lifted my spirits. One friend in particular was tremendous with you, and then I remembered the experience that she has had working and conversing with disabled people. She promised to come again to read to you, and as she moved away, you said, "Thanks." I'm not quite sure if that was a direct response to her promise, but everyone there thought so.

I arrived home at 7:50. The children needed help in going to bed. Because it's staying light later, it makes no sense trying to put them to bed too early. I went to bed about 10:00, tired and very low. Yet, I know who holds our future.

Your best friend

Reaching Others When You Hurt

Suffering confuses me deeply. Aside from my experience as a child, I have, for the most part, managed to witness suffering only from a distance. As a pastor, I now marvel at my ability in the past to deceive myself into thinking that I could truly come alongside those who suffer in their pain. I now face the honest truth that I felt relief when the day ended, and I could go home, close the door, and enjoy the safe haven of my home. My earliest experience as a pastor with another family's suffering began to shake some of my preconceived notions that God is predictable and easily explained.

I began my ministry in August 1985 as a youth pastor in a church in the beautiful Blue Ridge Mountain region of Hendersonville, North Carolina. Elaine and I had just graduated from college, and we began our ministry with a lot of theories but no idea how we would even begin to put them into practice. It did not help that I had been called to serve as a full-time youth pastor in a church with only three young people. Undaunted, I did all that I knew to do — spend time with the three teens and begin combing the neighborhood for other prospective youth group members.

One of the three teens was a young man named Rodney who had suffered from epilepsy all of his life. What happened to Rodney during our first year opened my eyes to the reality that ministry is not only a painful occupation but also one into which no one should go without a deep conviction that God has called him. Rodney and his family were pursuing a radical new surgery to cure epilepsy. This costly procedure, offered only in Canada, involved a precise surgery to remove from the brain the scar tissue that caused his seizures.

The church rallied around the family, supported them in prayer, and sent them off to Canada with high expectations. *God heals in many different ways,* we told ourselves. This time, He would heal Rodney through the skills of surgeons. Rodney came back a changed man. The surgery was a success, and Rodney would go for months at a time free of seizures. A new life was opened up for him, one that granted him freedom and a wide range of opportunities.

I finished work one day and was alone in our home when the phone rang. Don, my pastor, struggling unsuccessfully to maintain control of his shaking voice, informed me that Rodney had lost control of his motorbike, hit a tree, and died from the injuries. I was in shock. Surely this sudden twist in the family's life somehow had a divine purpose. Fighting anger, I accompanied the pastor to the hospital waiting room, where more than twenty family members were gathered.

I had absolutely nothing to say or to offer them. What do you say to a family who one week praised God for His provision of healing and now experienced a God who allowed this tragedy? I just stood there feeling extremely uncomfortable and out of place. Here was one of those moments when I could not wait to go home, close the door to my house, and sigh with relief that God had spared me such agony.

I confess that for years after that, I ministered to the dying at arm's length, a distant pastor who managed to give the impression that I cared. In my ministry in Texas (1989-1991), I stopped by weekly to visit Bob, a parishioner, who for five years had been fighting lymphoma cancer. Bob and his family lavished praise on me for my compassion and love. Even after Bob died and we had moved to England, I received phone calls from his daughter, who could not say enough concerning how we meant so much to her in their time of grief. What she and her family did not see were the many times when I passed Bob's house too tired to go in or too busy to fit a short visit into my schedule.

Just two months before Elaine's surgery, I believe that God placed such a burden on my heart for hurting people that I came close to ministering with a heart of true compassion. God would use another young man named Matthew to help me. Something about pastoral work in England did not leave much room for surface relationships and arm's-length ministry. The pain in people's lives seemed too real to me. As one of the only pastors in the local area, my role as a counselor and encourager had to be conducted with genuine love. God was truly giving me a love for people. I began to hurt with and for them.

Matthew was fifteen when he first began to visit our church. He came with his friend, Craig. They were an unusual pair. Neither of them had parents who cared about God or church, so Matthew and Craig had attended a church close to their home on their own initiative since the time they were children. Now, committed and hungry for deeper teaching and a larger church family, they came to us and were quickly embraced as part of the family. We marveled at their passion for God. I remember one day coming into the church and seeing Craig on his knees praying for the service that day.

The world finally got a hold of both Matthew and Craig, and it broke my heart. They left the church, and we did not hear from them for four years. Then one Sunday morning, they showed up. Both of them looked worn out. The spark and enthusiasm that once had distinguished them had evaporated in their years of living in the world. Yet, here they were at church. After the service, Matthew expressed his desire to return to church and begin giving his life back to God. He called me that week to talk about it. But it was not to happen.

That week, Matthew returned from college and, while stepping out of the bus, was hit by an oncoming car. I rushed to the hospital and sat with his parents, joining them in their grief. It did not look as though Matthew would make it. His chest was crushed, and his lungs and heart had sustained serious damage. Every day, the word was the same. Matthew was still in a coma, and they did not know if he would live.

I visited Matthew every day, not because I had to but because I wanted to. I cared for Matthew and cried out to God to spare him. I was certain that if God did, Matthew would give his life back to God. After a month of almost daily visits, I began to see improvements in Matthew. Within a few days, he was moved out of intensive care, and his recovery was rapid.

Several weeks went by. Matthew was released from the hospital, and I kept calling him. He was not easy to reach, but I assumed that the hunger for God that he had expressed to me on that Sunday and the subsequent accident would, without doubt, cause him to rush to church. But he never did. I later learned that the week Matthew was released from the hospital, he resumed his party lifestyle at the local nightclub.

I was crushed, but I didn't miss the irony. When I ministered from a distance, I was lavished with praise. In this case, I had poured my heart and soul into Matthew's condition, both physically and spiritually, but I was shunned. Even his family, whom I visited daily for six weeks, never expressed their appreciation. Yet, from this experience only a month before Elaine's surgery, God had given me a new and powerful motivation for service. Suffering would bother me more deeply. I could no longer close the door and ignore life's pain because that pain was now on the inside, not only on the outside. I was to discover that involvement with suffering sheds a whole new light on it. How easy it was before to say, "Oh, people suffer, you know, because there is sin in the world. People make bad choices, and of course, God causes all things to work together for good to those who love Him." Now, however, pat answers and easy explanations no longer satisfied. God's inexplicable dealing in Rodney's life and Matthew's refusal to turn to God when he was at death's door made suffering look so complex.

I read the Gospels, and I noted that suffering bothered Jesus deeply. When Jesus approached Bethany, where his friend Lazarus had died, Mary, the sister of Lazarus, met Him. She cried out to Him, "'Lord, if you had been here, my brother would not have died.' When Jesus saw her weeping, and the Jews who had come along with her also weeping, he was deeply moved in spirit and troubled. 'Where have you laid him?' he asked. 'Come and see, Lord,' they replied. Jesus wept" (John 11:32-35).

Jesus is bothered by suffering, because He Himself came to suffer. Jesus viewed the pain of humanity not from a distance but from the inside. "He too shared their humanity" (Hebrews 2:14). One of the essential qualities that made up His heart of compassion was His own pain. Now God seemed to be preparing me to live with a pain that I could not ignore. Never again would I be able to close the door and with a deep sigh mutter, "Well, I am glad that *I'm* not the one." Now I *am* the one. I shut the door not to run from pain but to be overwhelmed by it. My life will never be the same but neither will God's use of me. I have to agree with the psalmist's words: "It was good for me to be afflicted so that I might learn your decrees" (Ps. 119:71).

Chapter 9
Praying for the Boy in Mexico

Day 10: Sunday, June 14

My Dear Elaine,

Today, Dad shared about a man who, in deep pain over a tragedy, made a point of praying more for others who suffer than for himself. As Dad told me this, he read from a missions email about a boy in Mexico who was suffering from a tumor. Several times today, Dad reminded me to pray for "the boy in Mexico."

When I arrived at Walton with Mom today, the doctors told me that at 5:00, they had done a spinal tap on you to see if you had an infection. Your incision was draining, and a fever seemed to point to a possible infection. You seem to have meningitis but not the sort that people suffer from in the general public (viral meningitis), the doctor says.

(Later when I saw what this less common type of meningitis (bacterial) did to Elaine, viral meningitis might have been a blessing.)

Breanna also came with me this morning to see you. She cried and said that she missed you so much. This is the first time that she has shared her feelings. For the most part, the children have been strong. I sense that Travis feels the pain, but he covers it up and distracts himself by playing soccer and watching the World Cup. One thing that you're missing is the terrible weather. In the nine days since we have returned, the sun has shone probably once. It rains and is cold which is typical for June in England. I have to admit that it doesn't help the mood in our household.

I read to you several stories from Philip Gulley's *Front Porch Tales*. They are enjoyable. When you wake up and need encouragement and company, I plan to read the whole book to you. You are stirring and uncomfortable today, more so than before. Your eyes are open more than previously. When I say *open*, it is more like half open, and I don't think that you see anything. However, at one point, while we were in the waiting room, the nurse ran in and told us to hurry because your eyes were wide open. You looked at the nurses, one on each side of your bed, and smiled at them. By the time we got to you, however, you were fast asleep again. Next time!

You seem to be in pain today. I can see it in your eyes, and you're holding your head a lot. You're so wiggly. At one point, I held your arm down which really irritated you. You slapped me three times and said sharply, "Don't! Stop it! Stop it!" It is one time that I was glad to be slapped!

We returned home at 1:00 and had lunch, but I couldn't relax. Our grass is a foot tall, so I began to mow it. Dad plans to finish it once it is dry enough. I was so worn out this afternoon that I cried several times. Mom and Dad being here, I believe, has given me an opportunity for tears. Otherwise, I would bottle things up.

I returned with Dad to Walton about 4:00, and we stayed until 6:30. When we arrived, Dass and Jeanette were there, and John and Irene had just left. Again, I couldn't hold back the tears. Dass assured me that, with all that has happened to your brain, rest and sleep are necessary. I am so impatient and often think the worst. What if you don't wake up? What if you don't recognize me? What if you're a totally different person?

My answer to these questions? I would love you all the same.

Once we arrived home that night, I received several phone calls. Your friend Margaret Trees from North Carolina called. She had just heard about your condition. She was devastated. Your sister Kathleen called, and she will be coming but will wait until you've recovered some. My friend Martin, from the church, called after I was already in bed simply to encourage me.

This morning, my letter of resignation was read to the church. Martin said that you could have cut the atmosphere with a knife. As of today, I am no longer the pastor of Birchwood Evangelical Church. I have a new task – to care for my wife. I doubt that we will go back to the States in July; I suspect that we will need to wait until Christmas. This will be an adjustment for the children, but they will do fine. I went back to bed around 10:30 and prayed for the boy with a tumor in Mexico.

Your best friend

Chapter 10
This Side of Healing

Day 11: Monday, June 15

My Dear Elaine,

I dropped the children off at school and came straight over to see you. As I came to your bedside, the surgeon who had removed your tumor smiled broadly.

"She's doing well," he said. "The fact that she is speaking some and moving means there will be no major brain damage."

I now hold onto these words. It's funny how the little things that you once did so routinely and easily are now milestones. I brought you a T-shirt, and as I write this, they are cleaning you up and changing you. I can't wait to see you. I keep thinking about how only two weeks ago you were healthy and robust.

On our way to Germany, you were happy, laughing, and energetic. I look at you now and try to gain some perspective in all of this confusion. How can a person change so quickly from being healthy and strong to being so helpless? Two weeks ago, I marveled at your boundless energy; now we cheer when you manage to lift a hand three inches. In tragedy, the human emotions must adjust quickly, and thankfully, God has given them the capacity to do so. I tell people that God has made us with an unbelievable ability to adapt to pain. Eventually, the haze and confusion lifts to reveal a solid and firm foundation of faith.

I brought my lecture notes to study for my exam. I don't think that I have the mind to review, but I must keep busy. My mind needs daily exercise. (For several years I'd been working on my master's degree in Biblical Counseling, something I did not complete until 2014.)

At 10:30, the nurse ran in to tell me that you were sitting up in bed and wouldn't lie down. Sure enough, you were. What a sight! Your eyes were open, but you were not really awake. You were chatting a lot, but it made no sense. One thing you did – and I knew by the feel of it that it was intentional – was to lay your head on my shoulder, and I hugged you. A hug never felt so good!

Well, I need to pay some bills. I realize more than ever how much you do at home. I returned home at 1:30 and treated myself to two hours of soccer: England beat Tunisia 2-0. I've been watching some of the World Cup, more as a distraction than out of interest. This is an event to which I looked forward to for months, but now it means absolutely nothing to me. In fact, right now sports seem so temporal. I wonder why people give so much of themselves to something that tomorrow will mean nothing. Has suffering turned me into a cynic? I must guard against that attitude.

Mom and Dad both have their share of ailments this week, and we scheduled an appointment for them at the doctor's office. Mom has a bad foot; Dad has shingles.

Brett came home around 2:00 and was grinning from ear to ear. Spending all of his time with his friend, Tamsyn, has been a real treat. I am glad that life can be normal for Brett. It surely does not seem normal to me. Children have a way of adjusting to situations that completely disrupt adults.

Mom and I arrived at Walton at 4:30. When we arrived, Helen (the best nurse at Walton) told us that you had tried to sit up, and you again had your eyes wide open. I'm filled with hope, but I'm so anxious. At 6:30, the church council came to anoint you with oil and to pray for full recovery. I felt timid. After being the one who so often led such exercises, God was now asking me to be the recipient of the ministry of others. It was a humbling and moving experience to lay our hands on you. Andrew began, and each person prayed in turn. I was last.

"Lord, we come to You in obedience to Your Word," I began. "You instruct us that if there is any among us who is sick to call the elders. We confess our sins to You and believe that the prayer offered in faith will make Elaine well. I pray that through her recovery Jesus will be exalted and that, as she recovers, her life will become a much richer testimony to Your glory. Amen."

I know that your life will never be the same. Your testimony will have a deeper ring to it. Knowing you, you will seek the Lord and ask Him to use this experience to touch others. That is the real experience of healing.

Your best friend

My Struggle with Healing

I remember once preaching a really good sermon on healing. It had all the ring of truth to it and was received with enthusiasm and praise. I felt good about myself after that sermon, because I had wonderfully exposited a very difficult issue. I would not be able to preach on healing with such confidence and polished skill if I were asked to do so now. I do not assert here that I no longer believe that God heals; on the contrary, I believe firmly that God *is* able to heal. I am simply and honestly confused about why it so rarely happens. My belief seems to be clashing with what I observe. I prayed for God to heal Elaine, and later, when Travis was dying, we both prayed fervently for his healing.

Some weeks ago, an older married student from Toccoa Falls College took me to the airport. We had never met before, so naturally we began to trade information about each other's lives. Everything was going well, and I sensed that this would be a productive trip – until I shared with her about what Elaine had endured.

"Does your wife speak in tongues?" she asked me.

Suddenly, another conversation began, this one a silent one in the conference room of my mind. This woman then began to suggest that my wife would suddenly and miraculously be healed if only she would begin to speak in tongues. I could not believe what I was hearing.

Does God play games with us? Does He say, "I will heal you only if you can somehow manage to place yourself in the category of one of these faithful and highly spiritual servants who speak in tongues?" Is this what God is really like?

My first real encounter with the struggle of healing occurred in the first six months of my ministry as a youth pastor in North Carolina. One day shortly after we arrived, Don, the pastor, took me aside and shared that his wife had been diagnosed with lung cancer. He was saddened but confident that God was going to display His power in the church through her healing. I tried to affirm this hope, but deep inside I was attempting in vain to drown out the skeptical voice that suggested that it wasn't all that easy. I have seen so many people work up faith, convinced that somehow enough noise and claims of healing would convince God to move on someone's behalf. I was new to the ministry, and so I desired to join Don in prayer and believe with him that God would indeed heal.

Some weeks later, we met with the pastor's wife, the elders, and the deacons. I felt like a bystander as I was called upon to join these spiritual giants in claiming a healing from God. Would my lack of faith or my skepticism put a damper on the Spirit's power? The room grew quiet as the attention was placed upon the fragile figure of the pastor's wife, who was struggling to keep herself propped up in her wheelchair. For a moment, the silence seemed sacred as she shared with deep conviction that God had told her that she would be healed.

Wow! I thought. *Something is going to happen here.*

She quoted the famous words from Psalm 6:5: "'Who praises you from the grave?' I am no good in the grave," she concluded. "God wants me well so my life can be a testimony for Him."

The elders and the deacons closed in on that dying figure. They offered a prayer in faith and dabbed the oil on her forehead. I left that place with a deep certainty that God would heal her. He did not. She died a few months later.

Today, I am less confused about healing. What I mean is that I am more at peace with unanswered questions. I have also come to believe that God seems able to accomplish just as much – or more – through someone's suffering than He does through a testimony of healing. I have only *heard* of people being healed; I have never been a first-hand witness to a genuine miracle. When I say a genuine healing, I am referring to a serious ailment that is completely and visibly reversed with no possible human explanation.

Later, you will read in detail about my son's long illness and eventual death from brain cancer. Toward the end of his life, the doctors admitted that nothing more could be done for him. Now, if he had been miraculously healed from this, the miracle would have shocked the medical world. No recovery has been recorded for the sort of cancer that he had.

I believe that God chooses in this dispensation to glorify Himself through the suffering of His servants more than He does through their healing. Western culture denies pain, so *God uses it to confront us.* We do what we can to run from suffering, so *He crosses our paths with it.* People identify with pain; therefore, the strength and the resolve that they observe in someone who suffers and remains true and faithful to Christ has a deep and penetrating effect on their lives. I will never stop praying for healing, and neither will I cease to believe in the power of God to heal. But I base my confidence in God more on the evidence of Scripture than on the experiences and observations in my life. The testimony of God's power over death and sickness is well documented and anchored in the Scriptures. My confidence that God is able to heal is well grounded but *so is my conviction that He can work just as powerfully when we suffer and are asked to continue suffering.* The same God who gives grace to those who are hurting is the same God who heals the sick. In either case, God is the One at work doing what He wants and what seems best to Him. I can live with this assurance: "For it is God who works in you to will and to act according to his good purpose" (Phil 2:13).

Chapter 11
A Cruel Game of Waiting!

Day 12: Tuesday, June 16

My Dear Elaine,

Dreams can offer false hope – but only if one takes them too seriously. My dreams the last two nights have been about you. In my first dream, we were at Black Forest Academy, and you, having been in the state you're now in, suddenly sprang to life. In the second dream, we were all in the south of France, and there again you suddenly made a miraculous recovery. I will take these dreams as confident signals.

Our friend Heidi called at 7:30 to see how you are. She was on vacation in Greece when her husband, Mark, called her about your situation. All of our acquaintances have their own story of where they were and what they were doing when they learned of your illness. I often wonder, with this world of reality in which we live, of whom I will hear next who has faced a sudden accident. I remember as a child in Papua having a mission pilot stay with us overnight. He was so much fun as he kept each of us four children in suspense with various magic tricks. Several days later, we heard that his plane was missing. It had crashed in bad weather, and he had died. It's interesting how that one childhood experience often comes to mind whenever I hear of people I know who are suddenly killed or injured. It reminds me, I guess, how close we all are to death.

I remember also speaking to an elderly man in our first church in North Carolina. He confessed to me how in his seventy-five long years of life he had never experienced tragedy of any sort. What an exception this man is to the painful and brutal reality with which most people live! Life is rarely free of tragedy.

Breanna forgot her school bag this morning. I groaned over this because it meant that I would have to return when all of the parents were bringing their children. I have not wanted to mingle with people these days; it involves too many explanations. I'm glad that I did go back, however, because when Avril (the school principal) saw me, she threw her arms around me, her eyes swelling with tears. She has really taken up our cause in the school and the community. If we need to stay longer, she will go to bat for us to see that Travis gets a placement at Birchwood High School.

I arrived at the hospital at 9:30. When I was in the foyer, I again made a mental note that this was the floor I had paced up and down nearly ten days ago. I also looked at the wall against which I had leaned as I agonized over the prospect of your dying. It is a strange sort of déjà vu when I enter this building each day.

I couldn't believe it; you were sitting in a chair when I came in. You were sleeping but sitting up, nonetheless. The nurses said that you almost walked up to the chair on your own. As I sat next to you, you adjusted yourself, lifted both of your legs, and placed them on my knees. We stayed like that for more than an hour. I am amazed at the things you do without seeming to be awake. You drank your first carton of drink with a straw – still asleep. I thought, *If she can do all of this while asleep, imagine what she will do when she wakes up.*

Your wound is very infected, and that concerns the doctors. Dr. Miles, who gave me a horrible prognosis last week, was glowing this time. You'll be fine, he says. You should have no speech problem. He did, however, give me the histology of your tumor. It is a fibrotic benign meningioma tumor, which grows on the outer cover of the brain between the skull and the brain. A meningioma tumor can grow anywhere along the spinal column. It is a slow-growing tumor and has a possibility of regrowth; therefore, you will need to be scanned once a year. As I write this, I wonder what your reaction will be when you come to terms with all that has happened in these last weeks. It's a far cry from an abscessed tooth. How wrong we all were!

They just did a spinal tap on you (the second one in two days) to release the pressure around your wound. The fluid was not cloudy, which means that it is unlikely that there is an infection in the brain. It's more likely a local infection. Because of all the infections and antibiotics, it will probably be the end of the week before you begin to regain consciousness.

I had decided to leave around 2:00 to go home, and just as I began to gather my things, two more of your friends showed up. One of them, Jane, has especially been a pillar of faith. She has experienced her own moments of pain, which gives credibility to each of her words of support. She looked me in the eye and said, "Mitch, God will restore Elaine completely. You just be patient and trust Him." It feels strange to be on this end of things. These people to whom I ministered for six years are now ministering to me. I find such strength in them.

I picked Dad up at home to run a few errands. I went to the bank, and Dad picked up some medication for shingles. He jokingly says that he takes pride that his bald head is now covered by shingles. I tell him that every roof should be covered with shingles.

I took Brett and Breanna to Forest Park after dinner. The walk in the sunshine made my life seem normal for the first time in two weeks. On the way home, we met a neighbor. After parroting the usual update, I commented that, having preached so often about faith in God and trust in suffering, I am now experiencing it for the first time and that will give me a new perspective in ministry. I then commented that this is really at the heart of Christianity: God saw man suffering, so He Himself came to our world to experience suffering that He might help those who suffer. The suffering of Jesus gives God credibility. I have been able to share this on several occasions.

At 8:00, my good friend, Terun, the assistant principal at the high school, dropped by, and we had a pleasant visit. After putting the children to bed, I called Derek Thompson about our house situation. They seem to not want us to be under heavy pressure about the house. We are surrounded by Christians who are like the arms of God embracing us.

Your best friend

Day 13: Wednesday, June 17

My Dear Elaine,

I arrived at Walton at 9:00 again, and you had already had breakfast - some Weetabix, they tell me. Until today, they had fed you through a tube in your nose. I wanted to know how they managed to tell when the tube reached your stomach, so I asked. Simply, they told me. They just cut a piece of tube that is more or less the distance from your nose to your belly button. Not everything is high tech here!

You were sitting up again and a bit chattier. Two of your friends came by about 9:30, and when one of them spoke to you, you opened your eyes wide, smiled at her, and laughed. A short time later, our field director, Larry Carey, came. He stayed until 3:00.

Your infection has not improved. Dr. Miles is concerned, and there is a good chance of some post-op tomorrow, but they will try some different antibiotics first.

The post-op surgery sounds dismal. They will have to remove the part of the bone where the tumor was removed. This area of bone is apparently a feeding ground for the infection. The doctor's confidence that this is not a brain infection is diminishing. If they have to do the post-op, they would leave the "bone flap" out for six months. At that point, they would replace it with either an artificial piece or with the original bone. This procedure is called a Cranioplasty. My prayer is that the antibiotics will heal the infection. It is a very anxious time; yet, your progress has been encouraging.

You ate a hot lunch and a piece of cake today. You drank a carton of juice and half a container of hot tea. I once heard a doctor tell a patient that if he didn't like hospital food, he was too well to be here.

In my devotions today, I identified with Jairus from Mark 6. He was devastated by the prospect of his daughter's dying, and like any committed believer, he took his need to the Lord Jesus. He cried out to Him as I have for you. Jesus responded compassionately and went toward Jairus's home. Along the way, He was interrupted by a woman who was suffering from an illness not nearly as desperate as that of Jairus's daughter. Jesus stopped, looked to see who had touched Him, and responded to the woman. Nothing is said about Jairus during this interruption but no doubt his world was spinning. Word came that his daughter had died, probably as a result of the delay. You know the story. Jesus raised her to life. But like Jairus, I am helplessly subject to God's plan and purposes. Like Jairus, my faith will be all the stronger because of this desperate waiting.

The doctor intended to do another lumbar puncture and then a scan. (I call the doctor who does this procedure the "Lumberjack"). He did neither, however. They will be delayed until tomorrow.

I left for home about 6:30, tired and discouraged. Brett wanted to go for a walk, but I did not have the energy. Janice Collier of "Fizzy and Lizzy" (one of the Christian clowns who ministers in our church each year) called to plan a barbecue with us, not knowing what had happened. It was so awkward explaining everything to her. We agreed that it should be held when you get well. As I do every night, I called Walton Hospital again to see how you are. I mouthed silently the familiar words as the nurse spoke them: "She's quite settled." I do not want you settled – I want you awake!

As I lay in bed, I reflected on several of the day's good points. You laughed a lot today, probably out of frustration and some pain. It was not a normal laugh – perhaps a reaction to medication. Nevertheless, your clearest response to date has been laughter. I smiled and slept.

Your best friend

Day 14: Thursday, June 18

My Dear Elaine,

They promised a heat-wave this weekend, but there was no sign of it this morning. I awoke anxious, knowing that there was a good chance of postoperative surgery today or tomorrow. Brett wanted me to take him to school, meaning a later departure for Walton. He's been looking forward to today. It's Sports Day at 1:30. Unfortunately, it's been called off because of rain, but the children will walk to Forest Park anyway. Brett takes everything in stride.

They were just taking you on a gurney for a scan when I reached your room. Our biking partners, Steve and Eleri, arrived while Mom and I waited. It was nice to have company. Shortly after you returned, I was told that you would have surgery tonight. I had all sorts of questions. They will cut through the same wound, clean out the infection, remove the bone flap, and close the wound. Amazingly, removing the bone flap is not as hard as it sounds. Under that bone (skull) is a hard tissue core that protects the brain. Sometimes the bone flap is even replaced for cosmetic purposes.

In the foyer this morning, I met Dr. Ramez Kirollos, one of the neurosurgeons. I explained that I knew a former student of his, Dr. Julian Wong, who attends the Manchester Alliance Church. Julian was very helpful the other night over the phone. Dr. Ramez was very excited that I knew him, and it turns out that he, too, is a believer who attends a Greek Orthodox Church in Manchester. He answered a lot of my questions, and God used him to reassure me.

It is 5:20 right now. Ten minutes ago, they took you down to the theater to operate. I quickly phoned home and told Mom to get this word out and have people pray. Prayer has been such a vital part of this battle. The church, in particular, has learned a lot about prayer through this crisis. I'm trusting God that this is the last battle. Before they left, you actually looked better than any other time during the last fourteen days. Your color is back, and the swelling is down. You had no fever, and your white blood cell count was down. Your blood sample showed no infection. This is a good time to do the operation, Helen tells me.

I just read Ephesians 1, placing your name in each appropriate place:

- "God has blessed *Elaine* with every spiritual blessing in Christ" (v.3).
- "He chose *Elaine* before the creation of the world to be holy and blameless" (v.4).
- "He predestined *Elaine*…adopted *Elaine*" (v.5).
- "In him *Elaine* has redemption through his blood, the forgiveness of sins" (v.7).
- "In him *Elaine* was also chosen having been predestined according to the plan of him *who works out everything in conformity with the purpose of his will*" (v.11).

How encouraging to know that even this crisis is somehow integrated into God's plan and purpose. You – *Elaine* – are special to God.

As I wait, I find myself reflecting on some humorous things that have lightened these past weeks. Yesterday, for example, I came into your room, and the nurses had all been wondering if you do yoga. You sat up a lot, remaining for some minutes in the lotus position. I told them that you had other ways to meditate. Today, the nurse Helen, who is always calm and unfazed, gave a couple of exasperated sighs. I asked her if she were okay. She said that she had a headache, and I replied, "Helen, don't mention headaches around here."

"Yah, I think I'll go get my head scanned," she joked.

There have been many light moments like this. They release the tension. As another example, just before they took you away, Alex asked me if you were allergic to anything. "Only brain tumors!" I replied.

The visits of people seem to be timed just right. At times, I want to be alone, usually when things are tense; at other times, company offers a good distraction.

At 6:20, they brought you back from surgery, and the initial word was that it went well. I spent a few minutes with you, waiting to meet with Dr. Erik Valentine who did the surgery. Your whole head was wrapped and was a bit swollen. You were wearing a mask for fresh air. Last week, I joked that this oxygen was necessary because of the pollution in Liverpool.

Half an hour passed before Dr. Valentine came. Meanwhile, I had put together a lot of questions to ask him. He explained that he had removed a large amount of pus along with the bone flap, which was one inch by three inches. The bone flap came from around the temple area, behind a solid area of muscle tissue. There would be no visible mark showing its absence. They keep the bone in a jar until it can be replaced in four to six months' time. Without it, many patients suffer from severe headaches.

I left for home about 9:00. I feel as though I've fought the last battle. I hope I'm right. I'm filled with the realization today that you belong to God. You are His child, and He stands over you right now loving you. You are precious to Him. From the day you accepted Him as your Savior and Lord, He has watched over you like any shepherd does his sheep. Your situation, because you are His child, is not unknown to Him. He watches with deep compassion, providing and intervening, sustaining and caring as only He can. Invisible activities occur in that hospital room that would overwhelm us if God enabled us to see on that spiritual level. I am confident that, because you are His, He will not leave you alone.

Chapter 12
God's Precious Child

Elaine's Story

Tragedies have formed the context of Elaine's and my relationship. Jonathan's accident and then her own suffering from mononucleosis provided Elaine an unusual platform from which to fit into the British culture during our first year of ministry. But it was the tragic death of a four-year-old boy that brought Elaine to God.

I first saw Elaine at the beginning of my second year and her first year of college. She was only seventeen years old. I was attracted immediately to her spirited personality. Her blonde hair bounced as she moved enthusiastically from one person to another, smiling and laughing and loving each one. I stood at a distance admiring her, unable to fight off feelings of attraction for someone to whom I had not yet spoken. Because I had made a promise to God that I would not pursue relationships that summer but concentrate instead on my studies and preparation for ministry, I asked God that if He had someone for me that it would begin as a friendship.

One day, I was perched on my motorbike watching a soccer game. Elaine sprinted over to ask me if I would give her a ride over to the department store so she could return some dishes. Later, she confessed that the dishes were just an excuse for a free ride. In the months that followed, we would spend hours on that bike, and I would discover that beneath the enthusiastic personality lay dormant a storm of pain.

One day, while sitting on a bench, Elaine shared her story with me. She began with some family struggles and ended with her discovery of God's love only two years earlier, following the death of her best friend's little brother.

She had entered her teen years in subtle rebellion. I say "subtle" because those who knew her did not recognize that she was running from God. She attended church and put on a good face around her parents, but behind their backs she participated in activities with her peers that would have caused her family some concern.

The summer that Elaine was fourteen, she and her family were camping in Wisconsin. The family received a phone call from Elaine's good friend, Annette, that Annette's four-year-old brother had been run over by a car. Little Michael was riding his tricycle down their steep driveway but did not stop at the street. The car could not stop in time. Michael was dead.

Elaine's apathy toward God now gave way to anger. For two years, she harbored this anger until one night she could contain it no longer. Standing outside on that muggy night, under a canopy of stars placed there by her Creator, she admitted that she was standing on the wrong side of God. There, in tears, she gave her heart to Jesus, released all of the pain and anger, and began a new journey. These changes were still in process, and some of the wounds of her life experiences were still tender. But when we met in Toccoa, Georgia, she loved God and longed to serve Him with all of her heart.

She still had one matter to deal with, however, and it had to do with the ring that I had noticed on her finger. I did not realize, during those first months of getting to know Elaine, that a young man in California had asked for her hand in marriage.

God again intervened. One day during a chapel service, Dr. Paul Alford, the president of Toccoa Falls College, was preaching, and a simple statement from him pierced Elaine's heart. Her fiancé, Karl, was not a believer, so Elaine had been seeking God as to what she should do. Alford, not knowing what Elaine was going through, could just as well have been privy to her inner struggles. He pointed to his Bible and asked rhetorically, "Why do we ask God what we should do about something when He has told us right here?"

That was all Elaine needed to hear. This was God's voice, a clear directive that she should not continue the relationship with Karl. That night, she called Karl and broke off the relationship.

During this same time, I was getting to know Elaine quite well and was falling in love with her. I also knew about Karl but at the time did not know that this ring was an engagement ring. Now Elaine had ended that relationship, and one of her friends told me that she had done so because of me. Armed with this false information, I began to pursue her with resolute determination. She was free for the taking, and she had broken off with her boyfriend because of me – or so I thought. When she finally told me the whole story some months later, I was put in my place but pleased with the motivation that this false information had given me. I was always aware that there was one relationship of Elaine's that was more important to her than me. We always reminded each other of this. We belonged primarily to Jesus, and what we had with each other was an extension of our relationship with Him.

As I watched Elaine suffer in the hospital those first weeks, I always knew that death would not diminish the fellowship that I shared with God one bit. I would later discover that the loss of human relationships can actually deepen one's relationship with God. This reality does not come naturally, however. As humans, we are intrinsically tied to one another, and how we perceive ourselves is often defined by these relationships. We must be careful with this nature. When we lose someone close to us, we might lose the very thing that has given us identity. Consider again the powerful way in which Gerald Sittser describes this vacuum as it related to his loss:

> Loss thus leads to a confusion of identity. Since we understand ourselves in large measure by the roles we play and the relationships we have, we find ourselves in vertigo when these are changed or lost. I sometimes feel like I am a stranger to myself. I am not quite sure what to do with me....It is a new world for me, but I act as if it were the old one. I am not a husband anymore, but neither do I perceive myself as single. I am not a father to Diane Jane anymore, though I think about her often. I am not one-half parent team anymore, however much I would like to be....It is a peculiar and confusing identity.[5]

When Elaine lay dying on the hospital bed, and later when Travis was first diagnosed with his brain cancer, I ran to God. I would do the same in 2006 when Brett, my youngest son, was also diagnosed with cancer. (I'll tell more of his story later.) Although the setting of each situation was different, the words that I said to Him were the same. Against every emotional instinct and even against human logic, I told God that if they died I would be okay because I had Him. This was a spiritual response not a human response. Humanly, I wanted to break. Something in my mind made me think that I could not handle this. Every urge in me was to scream out, to cry that this was an injustice. I could not envision myself as no longer being father to Travis and Brett or husband to Elaine. But God's indwelling Spirit would not permit these thoughts. He massaged this anger and soothed my pain, reassuring me of His deep love for me, a love that meant so much at such a time as this. No man can utter such an expression of faith apart from the indwelling presence of the Holy Spirit. "In the same way, the Spirit helps us in our weakness. We do not know what we ought to pray

---

[5] Sittser, *A Grace Disguised*, 70.

for, but the Spirit himself intercedes for us with groans that words cannot express" (Rom. 8:26).

Day 15: Friday, June 19

My Dear Elaine,

Today is the fifteenth day of our trial. Brett woke up giggling this morning. He can't wait for school because today the children are to bring their own lunch. Your illness has helped me to notice the simple things that bring joy. Breanna will visit you with me today. Finally, it's a warm day, and it's good to drive to Walton this morning in sunshine. I am keeping my emotions in check today, knowing that I should not expect too much response. You'll be tired and suffering the effects of this second operation.

Breanna and I played a quick game of tag in the elevator and arrived in your room by 10:00. Have you ever tried to play a game of tag in an elevator? If you ever do, do it with a giggly nine-year-old. Imagine our chasing each other in the small confines of a moving box!

"Tag, you're it."

"No, *you're* it!" Laughter at a time like this is so good for me, and the children are giving me reason each day to laugh.

Five minutes after we arrived, you sat up, opened your eyes, looked at Breanna, and reached out your arms for her. As I fought back the tears, you embraced her tightly. I sat behind you and asked, "How about a big hug for me?" You turned slowly, put your arms around me, and gave me the smallest of kisses on my cheek. You recognized us (or so we thought), and that is the one thing for which I had prayed. After that, you leaned back and didn't move much.

I took Breanna back to school, had lunch outside with Mom and Dad, did a little gardening, and returned with Mom to Walton. You are very sleepy; I didn't expect much response from you today.

Last week, when John Rockley brought Breanna over while you were still in the ICU, Breanna and I went for a walk. Walton Hospital is an old hospital. In fact, next month they will completely close and move to a recently built facility called Frazeterly Hospital. When one walks around the huge complex of buildings that make up Walton, one notices certain parts that have become completely unused and neglected. On our walk, we noticed some steps down an alleyway that led to an open grate. We could see that it led to a tunnel system under the complex. Apparently, some teenagers use this for their escapades. It reminds me of the sort of place where the Ninja Turtles might have lived. I commented how dangerous this place would be if someone inadvertently walked that direction and did not see the open grate. Breanna's explanation was insightful. The hospital, she claims, has run low on patients and has deliberately set this up to injure more people to increase its clientele.

You just now stirred again and sat up. Dr. Miles came and suggested to the nurse that you needed to be encouraged to move. They set you in a chair, and you promptly decided that you wanted to stand up. I asked Alex, the nurse, if we could help you walk. With both of us supporting you, you took baby steps around the whole room. It was encouraging, but you would not open your eyes or show any recognition. I'm worried about that.

Your best friend

Chapter 13
Watching God Move

Day 16: Saturday, June 20

My Dear Elaine,

    I began my day with a cup of coffee outside with Dad. It was good to be out in the summer air for a change. I also needed this time with Dad to sort through my emotions. All of the distractions of these several weeks have not allowed me much time to sit and chat.

    I took Travis with me to the hospital this morning. It has been more than a week since he has seen you, so I encouraged him to come before too much time went by. I hoped this morning that you would be responsive for his sake, and mine of course.

    You were sitting on a chair again, and within several moments, you opened your eyes. Travis was slightly apprehensive, but you broke through that when you stood up, walked three feet toward him, and wrapped your arms around him. The two of you stood that way for several minutes. Travis took great pride in the fact that you hugged him but pushed me away. Perhaps you identify me with the nurses because I have grabbed your arm so often this past week to keep you from touching your stitches. In fact, one time when I did this, you looked at me frustrated and asked, "Why do you always have to do that?" Eight words strung together was an encouragement because of the possibility of your having speech problems.

On the way home, Travis and I made a "Micro Machines" stop at Dixon's Electronics in town. You might remember that he has talked about this computer game for some time now. He couldn't wait to go home and try it out. On the way, he commented on how good it was for him to see you this morning.

Around 1:30, I returned with my mom. You were sitting down, surrounded by some of your school mom friends. They told me that you were very chatty, smiled a lot, and that you even began to say what sounded to them like "This is like a PTA meeting." I don't really believe that is what you were trying to say. You had not seemed coherent enough for that sort of insight. You smiled and laughed on this visit. Your words are not clear, perhaps because of the inactivity in these last three weeks.

Perhaps there will be some speech problem; I don't know. I really worry about this. When you stood, you wanted to dance with Claire and then me, singing and giving the appearance of being drunk but in a pleasant way. Your improvement in just one day is remarkable. I praise our Lord Jesus for giving you back to me and to us – or should I say, sparing you for Himself?

Your parents called from Stone Mountain, Georgia this evening. Dad has business there next week, and they decided to go a few days early. Your family has been strong and faithful in keeping the communication flowing among themselves. They have known pain in their lives, and in the time that I have known all of you, you are the one who has been significant in holding the family together. Now their pain is for you. Kathleen calls every day, often twice a day.

Your best friend

Day 17: Sunday, June 21

My Dear Elaine,

It's the longest day of the year, and for some reason one hundred Druids think it is important to celebrate summer solstice around the ancient idol of Stonehenge. I began my day with the Lord, enjoying what has perhaps been my most meaningful devotion during this trial. I read from Mark 6:45-56 where the disciples, faced with their biggest storm yet, find their only source of help in the Lord Jesus, who commands the storm to be still. I've learned in these weeks that storms don't last forever; there is always a point when the fierce wind lets up. The wind seems to be dying down in our storm.

Today is also Father's Day. Breanna was in tears because she couldn't find the card she had bought for me. She unfairly blamed my mom for this, which caused a brief moment of tension. I told her that as disappointing as it was that she had lost the card, what mattered most was that she thought of me. This sort of celebration is not the same without you. You have always been so good in raising special days to their highest level. I think that the children will really miss you today.

I left for the hospital at 7:30 and planned to attend church this morning for the first time in five weeks. It won't be easy. You were sitting up in bed and reached for me when you saw me. You hugged me strongly and for the first time said, "I love you." You refused to let me go. There was a cost to this blessing, especially to my squeaky-clean Sunday shirt: you were drenched in the fluid that was seeping from your head, threatening to stain my light-green cotton shirt. You needed bathing as never before.

You've picked up a staph infection called MRSA. It is resistant to normal antibiotics and is a fairly aggressive infection, particularly for patients who are in serious condition. Dorothy, your new roommate, is very ill. I don't know what she has, but they have chosen to place you in isolation.

Attending church this morning was emotional. I felt like a stranger. John Rockley led. After fifteen minutes, he asked me to come forward to share a few words and pray. I needed to say something. After all, standing before me were God's arms which have held me these past few weeks.

My words were choked by tears as I thanked the church and gave an update on your situation. I also shared how God has used this trial to give me opportunities with others. For example (I didn't share this when I spoke because it happened after church), when I walked up our street, I saw a neighbor washing his car. I dropped by to say hello. He had not heard about your tumor. After we swapped some information, he said, "You know, Mitch – and I know what you'll say about this – but what has happened to Elaine is enough proof to me that God does not exist."

My heart broke at those words. There is no more logic in that statement than in a child's concluding that his father doesn't exist just because the child has tripped and sprained his ankle. At least I now know where Steve stands. He never revealed it before.

I have spent a lot of time recently reflecting on what you and I have done here in England the past six years.

Your best friend

Working in a Secular Society

When we began our ministry in England in 1992, I never would have guessed how God would bring me into contact with such an extremely secular society. I began my pastoral work with a simple desire for God to use me as He chose in this post-Christian culture. I was too intimidated by the culture and overly self-conscious as an American to know how best to serve, so I simply looked to God to direct me daily. Looking back, I stand amazed at what God allowed me to witness just by being in the right place at the right time to watch Him work. Several key relationships still remain etched in my mind as significant indicators that God was moving supernaturally.

The first significant encounter was with a young man named Peter. I first met Peter when there was an orange stuck between his chin and mine. We both were at the local school's family night, and a game had us racing another team by passing an orange using only our chins. In the weeks that followed, I would meet Peter daily on the school grounds as we picked up our children at the end of the day; this time, of course, the embarrassing orange was not between us.

We spoke about books. Peter, who loves to read, had just lost his job as a jewelry store manager, and now he found himself in crisis. Our common interest in books led me to recommend some good Christian literature.

Within several weeks, Peter began to attend church. His appetite for the Scriptures was insatiable, but I did not want to push him to make a decision for Christ because I knew that God was still preparing him. After the service one Sunday, Peter approached me.

"Mitch, when in the world are you going to push me to become a Christian?"

Peter was ready. That afternoon, he gave his life to God. That, however, was only the beginning of the battle.

For several nights in the week that followed, Peter phoned me, sometimes at midnight, looking desperately for release from what seemed to be spiritual resistance to his commitment. Having had little experience in spiritual warfare, I did only what I felt was the necessary thing to do and that was to pray. I prayed that Jesus would release Peter from whatever it was that was holding him. And He did. He was free. Peter became one of the most encouraging students in my ministry in England, and there were many.

The battle with the spiritual seemed to be the context of much of our ministry in England, forcing some to question whether that could account for what later would happen to my wife and son. One day, I received a phone call from a lady in our church whose niece was struggling after the death of two children in the span of seven years. We arranged to meet, and my first question of this young woman was what she had done to help herself up to this point.

"Well," she explained, "just last week, and almost monthly before that, I visited a medium to contact my dead sons."

I was shocked. This ignorant woman did not see anything abnormal about coming to a pastor immediately following a visit to a spiritist. In her mind, the two professions were just as credible and had equal potential to aid in her desperate attempt to find relief from her pain. I argued in vain with her that God was her only answer and that her involvement with spiritism was dangerous.

Another incident involving the occult is worth mentioning. A dear woman named Jane had come to the Lord through our church and expressed a burden for her two neighbors, both of whom were involved in spiritism. She asked Elaine and me one day if we would be willing to meet with her neighbor, Helen, who was seeking God. We met Helen in our living room, and what transpired is nothing short of dramatic and further proof of God's deep longing to involve Himself in the lives of people.

At first, Helen hesitated to tell us her story, but finally she confessed that she had been a practicing clairvoyant for seven years. We shared with her from the Scriptures that what she did was not from God and could have severe consequences in both her life and the lives of her children. Convinced that she was now encountering the truth, Helen bowed her head, renounced her sins, and asked the Lord Jesus to renew her. Helen became a child of God.

I have had several people question me about whether I thought that Elaine's and Travis's illnesses were a direct result of supernatural activity against us. I answer such queries only by saying, "I don't know." I have struggled deeply with the question; I am not satisfied with easy, clear-cut and simple explanations.

When Travis was first diagnosed, I remember commenting to people that I did not think that I could accept his situation as I had accepted Elaine's. Something about his sudden illness, coming so soon after Elaine's, did not seem natural to me. I resisted what was happening to Travis like someone recognizing that greater forces are at work. I was angry, not at God but at Satan. Yes, I felt singled out, and yes, I was convinced that there was some connection between our trials and the fruit of our ministries. Because I have little to substantiate these claims, however, I have chosen not to dwell on them.

When Elaine was still in the hospital fighting for her life, I read a commentary on the book of Job. It struck me that in Job 1-2, Job did not know what we know, that is, that his crisis was a part of a cosmic bargain between God and Satan. All Job knew was that he was hurting. In fact, had God not later revealed it to him by divine revelation, Job never would have known what we know – that his life struggle was a direct cause of supernatural bargaining. Rather than being given an explanation, Job was given grace to live through his crisis, and that is what I sensed God was asking of me.

Having an explanation for all of the things through which we have gone – whether from God, from Satan, or from simply being the product of living in a natural order that is corrupted by sin – should not be important unless God directly reveals it to me. He has not. Therefore, I choose to live with the unanswered questions while His provision of grace carries me. That grace is sufficient because it confirms that nothing happens without God and without purpose. I can live with that.

Chapter 14
The Fires of Sorrow

Day 18: Monday, June 22

My Dear Elaine,

    After a great lunch at home and a game of badminton with Travis, I returned to Walton at 3:30. You have been moved to isolation because of the particular strain of infection that you have. Sam is your *bodyguard* – I mean *nurse*. He is from the Philippines and might as well be your bodyguard with the way you keep grabbing at your bandages. He's after you before you can flinch. I've decided to leave it to him because you slap me every time I intervene.

    Upon reflecting over these past two weeks, I am amazed at how unaware you are of all you have gone through. One day, you stood at death's door, but God spared you, I believe, because of the prayers of thousands of people. Yesterday and today, you are awake – incoherent, perhaps, but nevertheless displaying your stubborn independence by wanting to stand up and walk away. You've always chosen to walk away from defeat. You have often said, "I hate quitters," and you frequently follow this statement by relating the story from your childhood of the time when a neighborhood boy named Johnny Pulaski called you a quitter. Your response? You walked over to him and beat him up. You're disoriented right now, but I can see in your eyes that same determination not to quit. You're going to beat this. I'm here to help you.

Mom and I are at the hospital. I've been here for two hours and have seen you for only twenty minutes. Washing you can take time, especially if you're not cooperating. I sat on the bed with you, and you gave me a good hug. It felt like you, and I know that some things have not changed. You keep saying, "OK," and "really?" You're not yourself, but after what you've been through, I wouldn't expect you to be. The left side of your head still has some swelling but much less than before. You look good. I brought some of your own clothes, and right now you've been washed and are looking great. I will shop to buy you some long T-shirts. The hospital pajamas are thick, burlap-like, cloth material, and you keep mistaking them for your sheets. It's funny to watch you struggle to put your top over you as if it were a sheet.

I've followed an interesting order of anxiety these weeks. First, I wondered if you would live. Then I wondered if you would awaken. Finally, I wondered if you would move. Will you open your eyes? Will you look at me? Will you recognize me? Will you speak?

As I sat on your bed and looked at you as you were sleeping, I found myself rehearsing our wedding vows. The phrase *love and cherish for better or for worse, in sickness and in health* had an especially meaningful echo. *This* is when commitment really means something, isn't it? I am committed to you, Elaine Grace Schultz.

As we face so much sorrow and suffering around us, the following words from Oswald Chambers's classic *My Utmost for His Highest* ring clear:

> My attitude as a saint to sorrow and difficulty is not to ask that they may be prevented. Our Lord was saved not from the hour, but out

of the hour. We say that there ought to be no sorrow, but there is sorrow, and we have to receive ourselves in its fires. If we try to evade sorrow, refuse to lay our account with it, we are foolish. Sorrow is one of the biggest facts in life; it is no use saying sorrow ought not to be. Sin and sorrow and suffering are, and it is not for us to say that God has made a mistake in allowing them. You cannot receive yourself in success, you lose your head; you cannot receive yourself in monotony, you grouse. The way to find yourself is in the fires of sorrow. Why it should be so is another matter, but that it is so is true in the Scriptures and in human experience. You always know the man who has been through the fires of sorrow and received himself, you are certain you can go to him in trouble and find that he has ample leisure for you. If a man has not been through the fires of sorrow, he is apt to be contemptuous; he has no time for you. If you receive yourself in the fires of sorrow, God will make you nourishment for other people.[6]

Your best friend

Day 26: Tuesday, June 30

My Dear Elaine,

    I decided to forego daily entries as your situation has become stable. I have chosen instead to do a weekly update. I also found reviewing the details of each day to be emotionally draining. This way, I can give you a general overview of how you've been and of events that have transpired.

    Today is my birthday, and any thoughts of celebration are for the children's sake, not my own. You have always made my birthday so special, and your present inability even to know that it is my birthday makes it all the more difficult. As I awakened Breanna this morning, she hugged me and wished me a happy birthday. I could not hold back

---

[6] Chambers, *My Utmost for His Highest*, June 25.

the tears when she said, "I really wish Mommy was here with you, Daddy."

Yesterday, on the way to the hospital, our car blew its motor. It lost power, then there was a little clanking sound followed by a couple bursts of heavy blue smoke from the exhaust system. Thanks to our roadside service, I was able to get the car to Rylan Rover and rent a little Micro, all in an hour and a half. The repair seems to be a major job and not worth the work. It's funny how, when I pulled the car over to the side of the busy road, I laughed. I laughed because I just could not get upset about this. Suddenly, the condition of a mechanical vehicle means nothing when you, only twenty miles away, are fighting to restore *your* body. We are so deceived in this society about what really matters. So what if the car blows its engine when your wife is fighting to stay alive?

Dump the car!

Save my wife!

I walked away from the auto shop completely oblivious to that fact that I needed to decide what I would do concerning transportation. Right then, I just didn't care. [It turned out that in all these weeks, I failed to take seriously the warning light indicating that the coolant was low. I noticed it but assumed something was wrong with the dash light. I'm sure this will come in handy someday as a sermon illustration.]

In the past week, you have remained in isolation in Room 5 on Sherrington Ward. On Friday, you were released from the high-dependency unit (HDU), and you are now under the care of the regular ward nurse. To ensure that the wound heals, they have placed a spinal drain in you to prevent the Cerebrospinal fluid (CSF) from leaking through the wound. The wound has healed well, but the fluid still bulges a bit around your temple area. The fluid finds the weakest spot to settle, I am told.

You are now walking, with support, around the ward regularly, and your legs are strengthening. You remain very confused, and you have yet to give any strong hints that you know me. The subtle hints, however, have been reassuring. About once a day you say, "I love you" when I express my love to you. When frustrated, you call me "Honey," and on two occasions you have called me – out of anger, I think – "Mitch." When you're awake, you chat a lot, but it doesn't make much sense. You do have a wide range of word usage, so it seems that speech will not be a problem; rather, you likely will struggle in your efforts to express yourself. You have what is referred to clinically as "expressive aphasia." (Again, how wrong I turned out to be. Thinking back on this incident now, I believe in my heart that I knew your condition was a lot worse than I was willing to admit.)

Twice in the past weeks you have pulled out the spinal drain, the second time only today. I am watching the swelling on your temple. Usually, without the spinal drain, this area swells quickly. So far today, however, it remains unchanged, suggesting that the body is absorbing the fluid effectively.

Dr. Miles was in yesterday, and he thought that, barring any further complications, you could be in Warrington by this weekend.

Day 57: Friday, July 31

My Dearest Elaine,

I am sitting in Room 1 in Ward 14 at the Warrington Hospital, ready to fill in the gaps of this long ordeal, which is now in its eighth week. The best way to illustrate your rapid progress, especially since you have come to Warrington, is to tell you something that happened to me today. As I was walking down the hallway into your ward, I was stopped by a rather short, young Indian doctor who, when seeing me, put his hand on my arm and asked me how you were. I then recognized him as the doctor who had first seen you when you were brought into Warrington Hospital on June 5, over seven weeks ago. He was also the one who tended to you during those long hours of waiting, testing, and scanning.

He shared with me that yesterday, when he saw the two of us walking down the hallway, he could not believe his eyes. After I gave him an update on events in Liverpool and the three operations that you had undergone, he then shared with me that the night you first came in, the medical team supervising you did not believe that you would make it through the night. As he walked away, his last words left me in tears and praising God.

"It is a real miracle," he said.

Yes, it is! I see it so much more clearly now. Your being alive is a real miracle. Your progress is a real miracle. God has intervened. God has answered those prayers of thousands of people. You are a walking testimony of God's grace and love. I praise Him for you.

Let me now fill you in on the past few weeks. After trying to reduce the fluid buildup around the wound area, the doctors finally decided that you needed to have a shunt inserted. This would be a surgical procedure during which a small tube would be placed at the end of your spinal cord to drain fluid into your stomach. The tube is permanent. I forget the exact date when that was done, but it went smoothly, and I can remember coming in to see you the next day and seeing that the swelling around your wound was reduced considerably. It struck me that in four weeks you have undergone three major operations, which meant a delay in your return to Warrington. You are beginning to walk more easily, and several times a day I take you around the ward. You chat incessantly. (I later learned from the speech therapist that that is normal. Because you cannot find the right words, you keep talking until you find the ones for which you are looking.) The improvements in this are daily.

When the day finally came for you to move to Warrington, I was thrilled. It happened on Saturday, July 11. I went home to inform Mom and Dad, and within an hour I was at the hospital, waiting for you to arrive at Ward B 17. At 3:00, hospital personnel wheeled you in, and though you looked scared, I think that you were pleased to see me. I might add, though, that a doubt lingers in my mind through all of this as to whether you really know me. (In fact, I don't honestly believe that you were fully aware of my relationship to you until you arrived home. Because I was with you day after day, it could be that you associated me with one of the nurses.) You settled into your own room, which happens to be in good view of the nurse's station.

Later that afternoon, the speech therapist Rebecca came. As she pulled out her visual aid objects, you were scared stiff. You did not impress her at all as you sat there staring, refusing to answer any of her questions and unable to point to any of the objects that she placed before you. I felt that her timing to do an assessment was terrible; nonetheless, it was obvious even to me that you need a lot of help with your speech and with all things cognitive. Two days later, they decided to move you to B-14, a ward made up mostly of very elderly stroke patients. You will receive better care here, they told me, but I was not happy with the change and made my feelings known. Later, I realized that my reaction was largely the result of fatigue more than anything else.

Your progress was good in B-14. I came to see you several times a day and brought Travis and Breanna in at least every other day. You loved this and responded well. Your occupational therapist (OT) was a very sweet girl named Sarah. She helped you with taking baths and by making cups of tea. She met with you every day, and again the doctors were encouraged by your progress. Rebecca also came in daily. Several times, you were just too tired to respond, and she left for the day. Overall, I was very impressed with your outlook and attitude; it was consistent with your personality. You were usually upbeat, and when you were not tired, you enjoyed laughing and joking with the nurses.

Perhaps one of the worst days in B-14 was July 23, our anniversary. I had hopes that a good response from you would ignite new feelings between us. To this point I was still not really sure if you knew me, at least consciously, as your husband and best friend. The day before our anniversary, Breanna and I went shopping in Warrington, and I bought you an expensive bracelet. I was apprehensive that morning when I came to you, but so were you. Later, I realized that your tense mood had nothing to do with our anniversary but with fears about returning home. We were already talking about your coming home within a week or so, and it became apparent that the thought scared you. Later, you expressed to Sarah that you were concerned about how the children would receive you, especially Brett, who had not been to see you in a month. In fact, at that visit you were not even awake. He refused to go to a hospital again after that.

Despite all of this, by the end of July 23, I was glad that we celebrated even though it was under less than happy circumstances. In years to come, we will look back and agree that even in the darker, more difficult moments in our marriage, we sought to celebrate the union that we share. You don't always have to be in a joyful mood to celebrate marriage. Even a hospital bedside can be a good place to tell your spouse that no matter where you are or what you go through, you are absolutely committed to each other.

Any discussion about your coming home soon seemed positive. The doctor, the OT, and the speech therapist all began to agree that you would be better off at home than in the isolation of a dull hospital ward.

On Saturday, July 25, you were to come home. I went home to get things ready. Brett and I bought balloons and a "welcome home" sign. At 2:30, a taxi pulled up our drive. I could see you in the front seat crying. I knew this change would not be easy on you. The first person you saw as you walked out was Brett, and the first thing that Brett did when he saw you was to reach out and hold you. The two of you sat on the couch holding each other for half an hour. It was exactly what you needed to feel at home again. I knew that things would be okay. With God, they always are!

From your best friend

Chapter 15
Coming to Terms with Change

Elaine would later tell me that she cried the moment she drove home in the taxi because she was terribly confused. Her mind somehow was still attached to a schedule based on our original plans for returning to the States. She had no way of knowing that it was late July, but somehow and unconsciously she knew that we were supposed to be in America. When the taxi pulled down our street, something in that final turn was familiar to her, and when she recognized our house, she broke down in tears. Having no idea what had happened to her, she needed to come to terms with her loss. She held Brett and cried. She was about to begin her own battle. We were happy that she was home. Elaine, however, was only beginning to understand that something tragic had happened to her. Her reference point would be different from ours.

The months that followed were filled with time to adjust to Elaine's being home and plans to return to the United States. We thought that a move to America would be good for Elaine because the provisions for her recovery would be better there than in Britain. I was ready to go.

To me, these were our last months in England. I went through the motions of packing most of our things for storage, but I had settled in my heart that we would never return. I could never imagine Elaine's recovering well enough. During those months, she slept probably twenty hours a day. Our first priority was for her to get her strength back. She had lost forty pounds while in the hospital, and I knew that I desperately needed to help her walk.

One day, while we were walking on a familiar trail just behind our house, I tested Elaine by asking which direction we should turn. She had no idea, and I began to see that her situation was far worse than I had thought. Her speech was nonsensical. She did very little normally. She did not know what to do with a knife or a hairbrush. When she finally figured out what a brush was for, she used the wrong end. The speech therapist came twice a week. This depressed me terribly as it highlighted the extent of her disability. She could not even identify her children when shown a picture. She had no idea what to do with a pen and paper.

In the early weeks, I sat down many times to help Elaine understand what had happened to her. I could tell that she had no clue about what I was saying. Three weeks after Elaine's release from the hospital, her sister, Kathleen, came to see her and to help in whatever way she could. She was great for Elaine. Only three days after Kathleen arrived, the two of them were upstairs in our bedroom, and Elaine suddenly broke down and cried uncontrollably. She continued like this for an hour. I assured Kathleen that this was what Elaine needed, but inside my heart was breaking for her. Years later, Elaine would share with me that this was the very moment when she realized for the first time that something was seriously wrong, that something bad had happened to her.

We left England on September 15. There was no sense of closure to our six years of ministry. I just wanted to get out and begin a new life. I was tired. I felt weak. I, too, had lost a good bit of weight and was still deeply concerned that Elaine did not know who I was. The recovery of her relationships would turn out to be gradual. It was not as though a switch was suddenly turned on and everything made sense. Her greatest struggle would be in balancing her own loss and the pending loss of our son. How she managed to do it, I don't know. I can only say that she is the most courageous woman I have ever met. Her depth of faith is remarkable.

Not long after our return, she had the opportunity to speak to a group of women from a local Methodist church. I had her talk recorded. Her final words reveal the heart of one who still struggles deeply with loss, but nevertheless maintains a deep love for Jesus, one that has increased in the fires of sorrow. She struggled in her own way to say something like, "I know when it is all over with, it will all be okay. When I die, the first thing I am going to do is give Jesus a big kiss. Then, standing behind Jesus waiting for me will be Travis. After I kiss Jesus, I will give Travis a big hug."

Her battle was not over. Neither was mine. Our hope was to someday return to Europe, but it was a diminishing hope. Elaine continued to struggle with severe limitations. She was only now able to read on an elementary level. This limitation would improve, but it would take time. She was unable to express thoughts on paper but managed to write single words. Writing would take even more time to improve. It was only when she began texting, seventeen years later, that I saw a breakthrough in her ability to write short sentences. Elaine had to grieve her own personal losses while suffering the intense emotions of losing her son. Sometimes I think that she did not have time to grieve adequately the death of Travis because of her own pain. Or perhaps the truth is that she had little energy to grieve her own disability because of the pain of losing her son.

We returned to ministry with a limp. Over the years, we have wrestled with God face to face. Just like it was for Jacob, this staggering limp will be a constant reminder to us that we are servants, and God is our Master. The joys of serving such a Master will never diminish, but the scars will remain.

I have shared Elaine's story. What follows is a journey with more pain. You will find in it less of a journal and more a cry from my heart.

Part 2

Travis's Story

Chapter 16
Uncertain Days

Several weeks before Travis was born, I wrote the words of the popular hymn "Because He Lives" in the front cover of my Bible. I was attending a men's retreat in early November 1986, just around the time that Elaine was expecting Travis, and I could not help but think that this song was for my family as eight hundred men sang out the second verse to that great hymn. Here are the words to that song:

> How sweet to hold a newborn baby
> And to feel the pride and joy he gives;
> But greater still this calm assurance:
> This child can face *uncertain days*
> Because He lives.
> Because He lives, I can face tomorrow
> Because He lives, all fear is gone
> Because I know He holds the future
> And life is worth the living-just because He lives.[7]

---

[7] John W. Peterson and Norman Johnson, (Grand Rapids: Zondervan, 1982), 238-239.

I wonder now if God was especially preparing me with the words of this hymn because they would come to mind often in the years that followed. The *uncertain days* of which the song speaks would become the days of Travis's battle with brain cancer. As I write this, we have just come through these uncertain days. Travis lived bravely and acted courageously, facing the unknown with a maturity rarely seen even in an adult. I write this with pain but also with pride. My son is no longer with us. God gave him to us, and God took him from us. He has received the reward of a short life well lived.

Travis never read these letters but other people may. I had hoped that he would read them years from now as one marveling at how God brought him through a dreadful illness, but it was not to be. By the time I was ready for Travis to have these letters read to him, he was in no state to absorb them.

I hope that reading this section will cause you to reorder the priorities of *your* life. Don't feel sorry for us when you read the journal. God meant this experience for us, and what God purposes for one person should not be pitied by another. My prayer is that you will close this journal mindful of what following Jesus really means. Perhaps you too, like Travis, will be able to say, "I would rather be with Jesus than be healed."

Chapter 17
The Beginning of Another Trial

Friday, October 30, 1998

A.W. Tozer once wrote, "It is doubtful whether God can bless a man greatly until He has hurt him deeply." I agree with him, but I don't like it. We have to accept many things without being asked to like them, and suffering is one of them.

A week ago today, October 23, 1998, my son, Travis Schultz, was diagnosed with an inoperable brain tumor. I tossed from one emotion to another trying to come to terms with this latest turn of events. How does a father and a husband deal with two tragedies in four months? First, Elaine underwent a life-threatening brain operation, which left her with severe fluency aphasia. About three weeks ago, I thought that I had finally entered that rare "peace zone" where my life felt normal, ordered, and content again. I was finally recovering emotionally. Elaine is finally interacting, and we have begun to pick up the conversations that we had put on pause four and a half months ago. She has now begun to share her feelings and emotions. Her words are beginning to come together. Life began to seem normal for us.

Travis's symptoms began just three weeks ago. He threw up often and had no desire for school. I pushed him, assuming that his struggles were emotional. Then at one soccer game, I noticed that he seemed sluggish, making careless mistakes as he attempted to trap the ball. With nine goals in four games, he'd been doing well. On Tuesday, October 20, he was hospitalized for dehydration. At the follow-up visit that Friday, October 23, our pediatrician, Dr. Beth Pinkerton (now a great family friend), arranged for us to see a neurologist. Within an hour, Travis was in Dr. Barfield's office. Several neurological tests later, a problem with the brain was suspected. An MRI scan confirmed the worst: Travis has an astrocytoma tumor on the brain stem. To operate would be fatal. To do even a biopsy would be risky.

So now today, Wednesday, October 28, our pastor Les and his son Philip accompanied Travis and me to Emory Hospital in Atlanta to meet the radiologist and conduct a simulation (head cast) in preparation for the treatment scheduled to begin next Tuesday. I asked some hard questions of Dr. Crocker, the radiologist. The answers were stunning. I learned that without treatment Travis had three months to live. Even as I write this, I can hear Travis guiding Brett through a game of Nintendo downstairs. My boy! A life-threatening tumor? *Am I strong enough, Lord, to go through this again?* I stand on the same promise as I did with Elaine's illness, but my legs are far weaker now. Thank God for so many Christians ready to hold me up. Praise God that my dear wife is here to share the pain with me. *Is this why you spared her, Lord?*

After the somber prognosis, Pastor Les reminded me that when he looked at the radiologist's name tag, he did not see the name "God" on it. *Lord, you wouldn't spare Elaine just to take away my son, would you? I cannot accept this. A sense of the enemy's fingerprints in all of this is so evident. I place myself under the shadow of the Almighty. Protect me there, Lord. Protect us.*

November 1

The other day, I put my arm on Travis's shoulder and asked him if he was scared of what lay ahead.

"No," he said confidently.

"Why not?" I asked.

His answer touched me and confirmed to me his place in God's kingdom.

"Dad, whatever God wants for me, it's really okay!"

"Why are you able to say this, Travis?"

"Because, Dad, God is in it," was his confident reply.

I am not able to finish this entry today. The pain is so great.

*****

When Travis was just a few months old, I sat down to write him a letter with the intention that we would not read it until he turned sixteen. I'm frustrated that I have misplaced this letter in all of the moves we've made. I suspect that it is tucked inside a box that is stored somewhere. I'm sure I will find it someday. Recently, however, I did find the following letter that I wrote to Travis at the only other time in his life when he had to be admitted to the hospital. In June 1995, he was fighting a high fever in a hospital in England. I wrote it with the intention that Travis read it, too, when he turned sixteen. Here is that letter, followed by letters that I have written over the past year during his fight with cancer.

My Buddy Travis,

When you were several weeks old, I wrote you a letter that I intend for you to open when you turn sixteen. I have misplaced that letter, but I assume that at some point it will show up, hopefully before you turn sixteen.

I am prompted to write you this letter on a day when I watch you lying on a hospital bed in Warrington, England. We returned today from a wonderful, three-week vacation with our family in Orlando. You had a great time there playing with your cousin Melanie. Most of your time was spent playing Monopoly with her. She won every game, but you didn't mind a bit. That seems to characterize you, Travis. Winning or losing matters to you but not as much as just having fun. You accept losing because you had fun trying. I love that quality in you, and it seems to develop more as you grow older.

On this vacation, you picked up some virus. We fought to keep your temperature down, but yesterday it reached an uncomfortable 104.7 degrees F. You're in the hospital next to me right now because your breathing has been very labored, and your temperature continues to be high. Although I hope that you can go home tonight, it will more likely be tomorrow. It is at such moments as this that I realize that my love for you is so deep. Everything else seems insignificant to me. I try to fight the tendency, but so often I am preoccupied when you children are around. The temptation to overwork at your expense is always there, but I would like to say in the end that I have resisted well. I hope, as you look back at our relationship, that you could never accuse me of putting you second to my church responsibilities.

Now that you are sixteen, I pray that your commitment to Jesus is strong. God will permit you space to rebel, but I hope that you will never do so. Teenage rebellion is, in fact, a misnomer. It is not a reaction to rules or authority; it is a cry for acceptance, a struggle to discover ownership of one's own identity. I trust that by now you have a clear sense of who you are without needing to look for yourself in anything other than what we have claimed you before God to be: "Man of God at the Crossroads."

Your best buddy

Chapter 18
Broken Windows

December 25 – Christmas Day

My Buddy Travis,

    I have put off long enough writing these letters to you. The week you were diagnosed with a brain tumor, I sat down to begin a regular journal, but I found that I did not have the emotional strength to do so. Several months before this, when your mother spent those two months in the hospital, I kept a daily journal charting her progress. It was a painful discipline but one that allowed me to dissect my feelings of anguish, hope, anger, pain, and love. She has yet to read these entries, and I am saving them until I think that she can absorb the words without too much pain. I did not want to repeat this experience with you. I knew that I probably should, but I couldn't. I tried one time, but I put my pen down, vowing to pick it up again. I guess the day to continue is today.

When I look at you today, it is still very hard to believe that you have a terminal illness. You seem fine, and apart from a slight limp, now hardly noticeable, you seem normal and healthy. In fact, two days ago, we played soccer against two other boys, and you moved well but sluggishly. It was so good to throw a baseball with you today, showing you how to use the new glove that I bought you for Christmas. You've gained ten pounds and look a bit chubby in the cheeks. Some of this is due to the lingering effects of the steroids. You are down to a very low dosage right now, and in two weeks you will be fully weaned from them.

I need to review the last seven or eight weeks. When it first became apparent that you had an inoperable brain tumor, I was stunned. In fact, no words exist to explain the depth of my pain and confusion. It was only two weeks before this shattering turn that my life, for the first time in five months, seemed normal again. Your mom was finally beginning to make progress. We were enjoying walks together, and she was beginning to interact with me. A breath of fresh, calm air was beginning to blow on me after months of being tossed by the swirling windstorms of your mom's illness. For the first time, I believed – yes, really believed – that life might once again bring me to a place that could be enjoyed.

I first began to notice that something was wrong with you when, during a soccer game, you did not trap the ball as you normally did. You had played so well in this new YMCA league, scoring nine goals in only four games. You then began to complain that your handwriting was not good. You also resisted going to school and seemed more emotional than usual. Then you began to throw up regularly, several times quite violently.

By late October, Dr. Pinkerton had you admitted to the hospital for dehydration; you spent a night there receiving fluids. When you got up the next day, your balance was way off. You walked as if you were drunk. Several days later, you were no better and again, for the fourth time I think, we visited Dr. Pinkerton. You could barely walk on your own.

Several tests concerned Dr. Pinkerton, and it was apparent that the right side of your body was weak and numb. She scheduled an appointment with Dr. Barfield, a neurologist in Gainesville, Georgia, and within half an hour, we were on our way. I knew that something was not right, but I was thinking that it might be a pinched nerve that had been hampering your mobility. Dr. Barfield simply asked you to keep your eyes on his finger which he moved from left to right. I was several feet behind him leaning against the wall and could see your eyeballs, flickering rapidly, straining to focus on his finger. It did not look normal to me. The doctor turned to me and in a too matter-of-fact manner dropped a bombshell on my life. "Mr. Schultz." I could tell he forced his voice to sound calm. "I can already tell you that Travis either has a brain tumor or water on the brain. We will need to conduct an MRI immediately."

An hour later all of us crowded together in a small room, the doctor kneeling where you were seated. He gently put a hand on your knee, turned to us and confirmed one of his suspicions. It was a brain tumor on the brain stem, an *astrocytoma glioma tumor*. Since Mom had her tumor operated on just five months ago, I asked him the obvious question. *When will you do surgery?* Another bombshell fell, this one causing my heart to fall into deep despair. "I'm sorry," the doctor answered, keeping his eyes now on you. "There is no way to either do a biopsy or surgery on this kind of tumor." He then looked at me. "He will not survive this."

The doctors made immediate plans to send us to Emory Hospital in Atlanta. Within an hour and a half from the time the scan was done, we were meeting with Dr. Patronio, a neurosurgeon at Emory Hospital. No surgery would be considered, he confirmed, and you would begin steroids that night and radiation treatment within a week or two.

We went home that day needing to absorb what faced us. The bomb had exploded. I had an important choice to make similar to the one I had to make as your mom lay on the operating table in Liverpool, England. I could either collapse in anger and bitterness or lean on the everlasting arms of my Father in heaven. You know, of course, by my example and encouragement, Travis, that I chose the latter option.

As a Christian, and after what we had already experienced, it was really the only choice. To choose otherwise was to deny the promises of God and to refuse His care, which we obviously would need for the months ahead. What good is it to place ourselves outside of God's protection during times of greatest pain? Isn't it when we hurt most that we need Him most? You know this. Ever since you were a child, when you hurt you came crying to me or Mom. Coming to us for comfort when you hurt was an instinctive reaction to your pain. So it is in our pain. I wish that I had kept a more detailed journal for the six weeks that we traveled back and forth to Atlanta. It was a ninety-mile trip each way, and most of the days only the two of us went. About once a week, Grandpa and Grandma took you, giving me a break.

The days when only the two of us went were wonderful. We talked, laughed, spoke of light matters, and often discussed issues related to the Christian faith. Your faith deepened in those weeks. One day, I asked you if you were scared or uncertain of the future. Your answer touched my heart: "I'm not really worried because I know God will do what is best." Your acceptance of this trial has been amazing. You never once complained, although in many ways you had a right to do so. One day in the treatment room, a lady who had been on steroids for only two days complained of the lack of sleep that came because of the drug. You spent more than six weeks on steroids, sometimes sleeping only two or three hours a night. Even your chubby cheeks did not seem to trouble you.

It's hard to believe how quickly those weeks flew by. When it was over, we tried not to drive more than three miles from home during the Christmas holidays. I was sick of driving.

Dr. Croker, the oncologist, has been encouraged by your progress. Unwilling to say that the tumor could disappear as a result of the radiation, he has admitted that, based on improved symptoms, the tumor has shrunk. You will be scanned in late January, and I understand that if any of the tumor remains, you will undergo chemotherapy treatments. I plead with God daily that this will be the end of it. I beg Him that you may live a normal and long life.

It is the nights that are most agonizing for me. I awake, not in fear but strikingly aware of the reality of all that is happening to us – first to Mom and then to you. I imagine life without you. I realize that the possibilities of that are so real. Words from the doctors are haunting.

"Three months without treatments and he would die."

"Few live past five years."

"Your son is very sick."

Why is it that these words echo loudest in the chambers of silence in the dead of night?

Yet my pain is not for myself. God has given me an unusual strength through all of this. My pain is for you and your mother. I hate to see her suffering, struggling with words that won't come, living with the pain of not being able to read or write. My pain is for what you might have to go through should God ordain it.

Right now, we are enjoying a respite. We have laughed and enjoyed family time, our home, and nice fires. You notice that I call this letter "Broken Windows." I'm speaking of the windows of my heart. I want you – and perhaps later, others – to view my heart and to hear the chords of my faith being strengthened in that pain. God has torn my heart this last year. He is hurting me and asking me to allow Him to do this work. I will not resist Him. May my example strengthen you, my son. My prayer is that you will read these letters later in your life as a healthy young man. If so, your life will have served as a testing of God's goodness, a miracle of His grace.

When you were born, we named you Travis Andrew, which means "Man of God at the Crossroads." When I pray for you, I envision a grown man serving God – perhaps as a pastor, a missionary, or as a deeply committed Christian. Little did I dream that it would take only twelve years for your life to reach this intersection, and neither did I dream that it would come in this form. I can only pray that God would use this for your good and for His glory.

Chapter 19
At Wit's End

December 27

My Dear Travis,

Tonight my heart poured out gallons of tears that spilled out of that broken window. Mom and I went to First Alliance Church tonight because our church did not meet. Now I see that God planned it so. Dr. Mangham, the preacher, spoke on Psalm 107 and about what to do when you are at your wit's end. What do you do when life's storms have hit so hard that you think you can no longer stand?

You cry out to God.

> Some wandered in desert wastes, finding no way to a city to
> dwell in; hungry and thirsty, their soul fainted within them.
> Then they cried to the Lord in their trouble,
> and he delivered them from their distress.

Surviving the Fires of Sorrow

> He led them by a straight way
> till they reached a city to dwell in (Ps. 107:4-7).

By the end of the message, I could hold back no longer. It was not the tears that tugged me forward but the Holy Spirit. It was the Holy Spirit, not the preacher, who called all who needed to drive a stake to come forward. Mom came with me, and there before two hundred people my heart was exposed, and the view through that window was for everyone to see. I'm embarrassed by it now but not for the commitment that I made. You see, Travis, I am afraid. I am afraid of what I might have to face – your death! I believe that God could heal you, but I have to prepare for it if He doesn't. My trust in God's power to heal is strong. His power might need to be there for our grief, not for your healing. I love the way Ronald Dunn puts it in his book *When Heaven is Silent*: "Faith is not necessarily the power to make things the way we want them to be; it is the courage to face things the way they are."[8]

Your illness is like reviewing the tapes of my own childhood. Do you know that you are the age I was when I fell ill? I've told you about it, but I don't know how much you have been capable of understanding. I was twelve when, while I was away at missionary school, I began to slip into what would become a two-year battle with depression. I was sick and wanted to die. My mom and dad took me out of school, hoping that the change in environment would improve my condition. The change away from my peers only gave me permission to collapse completely. It became apparent to my parents that I needed professional help. So my dad and I went to Australia. Like you, my life during those months molded closely with that of my father's. I think of our daily trips to Atlanta. I notice how you need me, look for me, and depend on me. I see especially how your sickness has affected my work. My parents left the mission field for, of all places,

---

[8] Ronald Dunn, *When Heaven is Silent* (Nashville: Thomas Nelson, 1994), 38.

Atlanta, Georgia, believing that they might never return again. I, too, because of your and Mom's sicknesses, wonder if we will ever return to England.

I also know that your sickness will shape a faith that will be much deeper, much more real, than if you had not gone through this experience. I wonder what sort of person I would be had God's hand not pressed me in those formative years. Already I see a sensitivity in you that I saw only hints of before. For example, this Christmas you were more interested in using gifts that you received to buy things for others rather than for yourself. I believe that, if God heals you, your love for Him will carry you into service for Him that will please both Him and me.

While speaking to my dad the other day about the master of divinity study I am currently doing, he began to chuckle. I raised a curious eyebrow, so he explained. It seems that a psychiatrist who saw me once told my dad that, sadly, they could expect that I would never accomplish anything beyond high school, if even that. Yet, look what God has done. The same God will do great things through you. Take time, Travis, to seek how God can use all of this. It's not by chance that you have a brain tumor. It is by God's design. I don't necessarily believe that He put it there, but He allows it to exist, to grow, and to affect you. Just like Mom's tumor, yours, too, is for His glory. Strange, isn't it? A tumor for God's glory!

Colossians 1 tells us that our Lord Jesus "holds all things together." Nothing slips from His grasp. Nothing happens without His permission and without His need for it. He needs what has happened to you, Travis, so give your life to Him. Humble yourself before Him and say, "Lord, here I am. Use me." Let Him take something as ugly and as horrible and as deadly as a brain tumor, and He will bring glory to Himself from it.

What a God!

Your best buddy

Chapter 20
Watching God Move Again

April 12

My Dear Travis,

You and I sat down together and decided to keep a list of what we called "God moves," things that we see God doing through your illness. We talk so much about God and your faith. Nothing gives me greater joy than spending time reading your devotional book to you and then one day coming to your room and seeing you doing it yourself. All that I have sought to model in the Christian faith you are now making your own.

Several months have now passed since your latest scan. That scan gave us reason to rejoice because the tumor had shrunk about 30 percent. The doctor who has overseen your treatment even allowed himself to smile, something that I assume he reserves for special occasions such as this. At the Egleston Children's Hospital at Emory, where you were scanned that day, they called it a *good brain tumor* day.

More than three hundred children under their care are suffering from some kind of brain tumor.

A clown entertained children in the waiting room, and you loved it. He performed some tricks that left you baffled. Since then, you yourself have taken on an enthusiasm for illusion and card tricks. For some reason I was angry at that clown. I struggled to laugh, even though you did. I think I had a hard time reconciling the reality of your terminal illness, while leaving some room open for fun. It's just where I'm at, I guess.

We left the hospital that day, February 4, encouraged, and I felt lighter than I had in months. I think that only then did I begin to realize the weight of this burden on me. Many nights I awoke, shaking off a deep pain for you that overwhelmed me. God lifted that pain right off of me that day and placed it upon His own Son. His burden is light. He tells us that when we are burdened and heavy laden to come to Him, and He promises to give us rest. I need that rest. Recently, I read words from Charles Spurgeon's final sermon. What he said about Jesus has meant so much to me these months. I think you'll love them, too:

> He is the most magnanimous of captains. There never was his like among the choicest of princes. He is always to be found in the thickest part of the battle. When the wind blows cold, he always takes the bleak side of the hill. The heaviest end of the cross lies ever on his shoulders. If he bids us carry a burden, he carries it also. If there is anything gracious, generous, kind, and tender, yea lavish and supernatural in love, you always find it in him. These forty years and more I have served him, and I have nothing but love from him. I would be glad to continue yet another forty years in the same dear service here below if it so pleased him.[9]

---

[9] Charles H. Spurgeon, *Morning and Evening* (Nashville: Thomas Nelson, 1994), iii-iv.

Surviving the Fires of Sorrow

How good it is to see how much you have improved. At first, the signs were slight, but in time your walk improved, as did the use of your hands. You have established a solid reputation in the YMCA soccer league, scoring three goals your first game, two in the second, five in the third, and two in the fourth. It's not the goals, however, that please me. It's noting how well you're doing.

Your best buddy

Chapter 21
God, What Are You Doing?

May 20

My Buddy Travis,

You were scanned again on May 6. You have done well physically and in every other way, so most of me expected a good report but how good? How much did the tumor shrink? Is it slowly growing back? These questions do not haunt me, but they are ever present, constant in my thoughts.

The routine was similar to last time. We arrived early. You had the scan. We spent the day with some friends in North Atlanta and returned that afternoon after an anxious wait. Dr. Petronio, the surgeon who first saw you, was the one we met. He was impressed. I looked for the first hints of reaction to figure out what he knew about the scan. Finally, after checking you, he told us, "The scan shows 30 percent more shrinking from the previous scan."

That puts it at about 60-70 percent gone. Was he giving false hope? He kept placing emphasis on the word *if*. *If* the tumor grows back. *If* this even continues to be a problem. Such hope in such a small word. There are no *ifs* in God's vocabulary.

Travis, the Lord Jesus knows exactly what He is doing in your life. I live with that certainty, and I pray the words of Ephesians 1 daily for you: that you would live what God has *chosen you to be, holy and blameless; that you continue to grow in your faith; and that you become more and more like Jesus.* You have your devotions daily. Yesterday, I entered your room and was pleased to see you lying on the bed with your Bible open before you. Looking up at me, you said, "Dad, I am doing this for Jesus, not for you."

We worked together on constructing a sermon from Psalm 23 this morning. He is our Shepherd. And what will the aim of the sermon be? To share with others in what way He is our Shepherd. Then we looked at how the passage addresses that issue. You reminded me again that you want to be a preacher when you grow up.

Recently, Mom spoke to a thousand women at a ladies retreat, giving a five-minute testimony. Imagine that! Just months ago, she could say so little. We are proud of her, aren't we? She works so hard. She's so determined. She wants it so badly. I don't know if you children understand the pain that I carry for her. My heart aches daily, and sometimes it is almost unbearable. I want her to read. I want her to write. Yet, I accept who she is and the way she is. Having said this, I add that she continues to progress so well. I have never met a woman with such courage. Her love for Jesus is so real, and her faith is so strong. This love and courage comes from acceptance.

Acceptance is needed in the pain, Travis. Without acceptance, we fight God. We do not need to fight Him. We need Him. The presence of Jesus has been so real this year. I would not know Him as I do without this trial. Do you understand now why James urges us, "Consider it all joy when we face trials of many kinds" (James 1:2)? We have to acknowledge it, don't we? Pain does draw us closer to Jesus. It's true. It's real. It works. Praise His name!

After Job had suffered terribly, he recognized that his view and understanding of God had been vague and distant. His suffering pried open a window revealing God in a new way. Note what he says. Reflecting on his past, he remarks, "My ears had heard of you but now my eyes have seen you" (Job 42:5). We don't like it, but God uses pain as one of the greatest vehicles whereby He reveals Himself to us. Why? Well, because pain forces us to acknowledge that we are not really as much in control of our own lives as we previously thought. It's easy for those who do not suffer to be self-sufficient, to rely on their own abilities, and to feel that they do not need God. They think that they are managing quite well without Him. However, when the storms of life hit, they are not able to stand so confidently on their own. Suddenly, they need someone else's help. I have yet to meet a Christian who did not say that suffering brought him or her into a deeper union with God.

In early May, we spent a weekend with your Aunt Ruthy and her family in Florida. This was so good considering your last trip there. Back in December, you could hardly move, and you slept most of the time. On Sunday, we went to Tallahassee, and I spoke at church. You told me afterwards that I did a really good job. I noticed that when I explained to the congregation what you are going through, you wiped tears from your eyes.

You have a motorcycle now. Yesterday, I bought a Yamaha 100, a nice trail bike that is also street legal. It was such fun to ride with you. I hope that we can go to a bike trail soon and really put it to the test.

Your buddy forever

P.S. Oh yes, just for the record: in seven soccer games, you have scored seventeen goals. What a guy!

June 4

My Buddy Travis,

In my despair, prayer has been my only effective outlet. I have prayed as never before. I wrote the following prayer in Lexington, Kentucky, as we were en route to Indiana. Mom and I just got back from our mission's annual convention in Portland. We left you in Georgia, confident that you were doing well. In fact, on the following Sunday, before three thousand people, I gave testimony of how God was healing you. The morning after we got back, my heart sank when I saw you hobble slightly as you walked down the hallway to greet me. Although I did not want to acknowledge it then, I knew deep in my heart that your symptoms were coming back. Here is what I had to say to God.

"Lord Jesus, the psalm I read this morning (Psalm 126) is a cry for heaven. It is appropriate that You lead me to drink from the well of this psalm this morning, nearly one year to the day after Elaine's surgery. According to Your Word, 'The Lord has done great things for us, and we are filled with joy' (v.3). Entering Zion, following a life sown in tears, is a reward for the pain. The price for patience and endurance will be unspeakable laughter and joy. As it says in this psalm, 'We were like men who dreamed. Our mouths were filled with laughter, our tongues with songs of joy' (v. 1-2).

"Thank You, Lord, for what You have taken me through this last year. I would not have chosen such a path if my destiny lay in my own hands. I would have chosen a path paved with ease and comfort, a path the surface of which was level and smooth. Your path for me has strengthened me. Your path has led me toward You. I have not had to walk much on this path because as I stumbled, You carried me. O Lord Jesus, give me endurance if You choose to keep me on this path. You know my concern for Travis this week. Once again, he seems to have weakened. I try to shrug off the possibility that the tumor has regained a new vigor, but I can't.

God, You are *Jehovah Rapha*, the Great Physician, and Your hand has been there all of the time. O God, heal and restore, I pray."

Your best buddy

Chapter 22
Unexpected Bends

June 19

My Dear Travis,

There are many bends in this road of life that surprise us. In this past year, we have reached some bends that reveal encouragement and joy. Here the path seems level, and the scenery is breathtaking. We have praised God and thanked Him for His mercy as we sat and caught our breath. Other bends, however, have offered us the disappointing sight of more dark valleys and difficult terrain. Here we feel a heaviness, as though the hand of God were pressing on our soul. We don't notice the scenery as much on these bends because our thoughts are consumed by the pain and difficulty of the journey. It is such a bend that I feel we are on again.

Within a week of coming home from Portland, it was obvious that the symptoms we thought were long gone had returned. Eager for our vacation to Indianapolis, we went ahead in spite of the concern. By that Monday, though, we realized that the problem would not go away on its own, so we made an appointment with a doctor at Riley Hospital in Indianapolis. This is the same hospital where your cousin Sarah has received much of her treatment for cystic fibrosis. They scanned you, looking for a buildup of fluid on your brain. They found none. We went ahead with our camping trip. You managed well but sluggishly. Meanwhile, the uneasiness in me only increased. While the doctors detected nothing, I was bracing myself for the next phase of the battle.

Only when we arrived in Toccoa did my worry for you reach new heights. We took you to Emory on the Friday we returned. A scan found that your ventricles were enlarged with fluid, causing pressure to build up in your brain. Once again, I took this need to God. Yesterday, I wrote the following prayer, bringing my plea to our Heavenly Father.

"O Lord, Travis's symptoms have returned. Three days now, Lord, I have wrestled with You as I never have in my life. I cannot understand what is happening; neither can I understand how You allow us to undergo so much emotional turmoil and so many uncertainties. The surgeons cannot believe that the tumor has returned since the last scan. O God, may the news we receive today be in our favor, I pray. In Your mercy and grace, do not ask us to go through more than we have already. Yet, yesterday on a walk, I gave it all to You. I turned over my anger to You and confessed my doubt in Your sovereignty. I told You that I would willingly accept whatever You had planned, and within minutes Your Holy Spirit poured over me like a fresh wave. Oh, thank You for the endurance that You give in suffering. I have asked two things of You and two alone: that, whatever happens, You would give us the grace to accept it and the grace to endure it. As *Jehovah Jireh*, I know that You will provide.

"I have reflected a great deal on Abraham lately, particularly in the last days. What were You asking of Abraham? It must have been far more than a willingness to give up his son. Abraham, I have come to see, was asked to surrender *himself* unequivocally to You. This was a test of obedience. No! It was the *making* of obedience. Was Abraham personally willing to be so obedient that he would submit himself to do anything that You asked him to do, even if it went completely against logic and reason? You were not looking for Isaac on that altar that day; You were looking for Abraham.

"Like Abraham, my own life has been tightly woven with my son's life. Ever since Travis was born, I see that my own life, my own childhood has been projected on him. That first day at school, at age five, when he cried and screamed, pulled deep from within me a flood of memories of my own experience of being sent away to boarding school. This latest trial seems in so many ways to parallel what I went through exactly at the age that Travis is now. O God, You are not asking for Travis; You're asking for me to be on that altar.

"Last night, You heard Elaine and me talking. I said to her, 'Do you sometimes think we will have only two children?' O God, may we live to see our children grow up. Thank You for Psalm 128:3-6: 'Your wife will be like a fruitful vine within your house; your sons will be like olive shoots around your table. Thus is the man blessed who fears the LORD....and may you live to see your children's children.'

"Abraham's willingness to give up his son revealed a heart that was completely and totally devoted to You. His life, Your covenant, was completely wrapped up in that boy. Yet, Abraham did not allow the illogic of what You asked of him to hold him back. In faith, he trusted You, and Lord, I want to say right now that in faith I trust what You are doing. Amen."

Your best buddy

Chapter 23
Preparing for a Battle

June 21

My Dear Travis,

    Sometimes I do wonder if our trials are due to my sins or any particular sin. I suspect that some people out there perhaps silently wonder about that, too. Have I ever thought this of others while I have observed them suffering? I hope not. Yet, it is a natural human response to crisis. Particularly in this culture, we need an explanation for everything that happens to us. That is why people in American evangelicalism, it seems, are quick to look for the blessings that come from pain. A believer dies, and very quickly we begin to hear reports of "the amazing way God has used this." We cannot accept that some of the things that happen to us have a mysterious and unexplained element to them.

    Let's go back to the issue of my sin. I have prepared myself with a response if someone ever asks me if I think that my sins were the cause of the crisis that we have experienced. My response? "Which sin? God would have a table full from which to choose, and He would have the right to punish me for any of them. If it is my sin that has caused this, I must say to God, 'Lord, I deserve it, but have mercy, Lord.' Are we not all sinful? If I am being punished, why do so many others seem to get away with so much more?"

Your best buddy

June 22

My Dear Travis,

Today – in fact, right now at 7:30 in the morning – you are in the hospital recovering from surgery to insert a shunt to relieve the pressure. I've not seen you today, but we will go over in half an hour. Mom and I are staying at the Ronald McDonald house just one-half mile from Emory Children's Hospital, where hopefully you are resting quietly in Room 596.

Mom and I meditated on 1 Peter 1 this morning. We prayed together that we would all be "shielded by His power." This thought especially encouraged Mom, and you should have heard her pray. She went on for more than five minutes, and Travis, it touched me deeply. It's really hard to know what this is like for her. I don't see Mom reacting as she would have before to something like this. She is still numb and tires easily. Sometimes I wonder if she is really able to absorb everything that is happening to you. When you were first scanned on that day we took you to Gainesville, not until you were lying in the MRI machine do I think that it struck her what you had. I noticed that she just sat there staring as we waited for your MRI to be complete. I came over to her and shouted over the noise, "Do you understand what Travis probably has?"

She looked at me, and I repeated myself. "We think he has a brain tumor," I screamed. At this, her face turned white, and she began to cry. My heart broke for her. Yet, she has not been able to share her deep feelings with me. She can't. Her words are so few, and she still seems so limited in her ability to understand things. I even wonder if she would have taken this harder had she not gone through this herself.

Travis, our hearts are heavy, but our trust in Jesus remains strong. The last scan, taken on Friday, shows some activity with the tumor. They tell us that it is a cyst, and despite their hope that the shunt will relieve you, I have a gut feeling that it might be related to the tumor. If this is so, you are in for the battle of your life.

I am spending a lot of time preparing myself for this battle. It is hard to know, Travis, how to prepare for a battle that we all know could involve death. Battles can be won only when attention has been placed on preparation. In my weakness, my strength comes in trusting the Lord Jesus. Trust is such a vital subject these months. I often tell Jesus, "I trust You." I have to state this if I truly believe that He knows what He is doing. What I am trying to say, Travis, is that *we prepare for battles by trusting the One who fights for us*. Jesus has made a lot of promises that apply in times of crisis. It is our part to trust that He will do what He says.

I have no idea what lies ahead. I feel numb in many ways but at peace in other ways. There are times, though, when I wonder if I am confusing peace with numbness. What I know is that I am not alone. Mark's record of Jesus' agony in the Garden has given me courage to face what I know is sure to happen.

Your best buddy

Chapter 24
The Letter I Never Wanted to Write

June 26

My Dear Travis,

    We're sitting on the deck together, talking and reading. I had my devotions before you awoke, and you joined me half an hour ago. I am encouraging you to read more as a way to keep yourself busy and so, as I always tell you, your brain won't turn to mush. I realize that you are suffering from double vision, although you do not talk about it very often. I am still amazed at how little you complain. I heard recently of a boy who needed scanning for a tumor. The parents had to restrain him because he was so scared. Not once have you uttered frustration over all that you are going through. You and your mother have a lot more in common than just your blue eyes.

You came through your shunt surgery well. You came home Tuesday and are trying to regain your strength. Your balance is no better. I have to conclude that your symptoms are either caused by the cyst or your tumor. I sense that it is because of the tumor. I know what this means, and I am deeply worried. Mom and I go through so many emotions: fear, trust, peace, uncertainty. This is when faith and trust mean the most, Travis.

I told you yesterday about the cyst. I realized that you would begin to wonder why the symptoms are no better, so I explained this other problem to you. Several hours later, I came downstairs, and you looked so depressed. You began to cry. We talked and prayed. You need these moments, but it is hard for me to see you suffer this way. It brings back so many memories of when I was sick at your age. I shared with you how I read to keep my mind off my pain. This was also a time when my trust in the Lord deepened. Like you, I did not have many friends around. It was a lonely time but a time when I learned to live independently. I learned to value solitude and time with my family. Yesterday, when I picked up Breanna from the Crosby's, the youth group was gathering for a swim party. I could sense the heaviness of your heart as you saw others doing things that you cannot do. But again, you said nothing.

In the last several days, your *What Would Jesus Do* (WWJD) devotional has focused on finding a treasure. A person finds treasure in a field and sells all that he has to buy the field so that the treasure can be his. We must give up all that we have to gain the kingdom of God. Today, the story was about a boy who searched for treasure for years and found little, until one day he found a rich deposit. I asked you for an application to your life, and you explained to me that it is like the Christian life. It can be boring, uneventful, and sometimes painful, but when you die and get to heaven, you find a wealth of treasure.

Your best buddy

July 9

This prayer is what I wrote today as the pain became too great to keep to myself.

"Dear Lord,

What You are asking us to go through hurts. We are told that Travis might have only months to live. O God, does it have to be this way? Can there be another way? He has become so weak, and now, only a few weeks after his symptoms returned, he can hardly walk. O Lord, have mercy. He is only twelve. I cried out to You at his bedside last night and pleaded with You to heal him. Why do I struggle believing that You will do it? No! It's Your will with which I struggle, not Your ability. I know that You can do it; my fear is thinking that You probably won't. Please, Lord, do not let that unbelief keep You from demonstrating Your power over Travis's sickness.

"I try to imagine life without Travis, and O God, it hurts. Your peace carries me, but deep inside, Lord, I am so afraid. I trust You, Lord. I believe completely that You are doing what is best to reveal Your glory. I see how this is already bringing glory to Your name. My own faith is being stretched. My love for family has deepened. The church has rallied so faithfully around us. People are moved by our strength and trust in You. Lord, it still hurts. Imagine, Lord, what healing would do. Yet, You do not need to prove Yourself. You do not need Travis's healing – but, Lord, I plead and appeal to Your mercy. In Your mercy and great compassion I ask, Lord, for a miracle.

"I pray for Brett and Breanna. O God, have mercy on them. Whatever You choose to do with Travis, my prayer is that at least, Lord, You will place a hedge of protection around those two children. There are angels in heaven who protect little ones. May Your angels come closer to these two children and provide the care, encouragement, and understanding that they will need.

"And, O Lord, help Elaine. Thank You for the miracle that You are doing in her life. Encourage her today. My prayer is not just for healing but for support to her weak spirit and hurting soul. Place Your reassuring hand upon her life. Help her to see You clearly, to discern Your presence in the midst of her confusing and hurting world."

July 10

My Dear Travis,

This is the letter that I knew I might have to write you some day. I have not wanted to write it, but I know that I must.

You are dying, Travis. I don't know how many more of these letters I will write. Your symptoms have worsened, and a little more than a week ago, we learned that your tumor has begun to grow. The surgeon in Atlanta told us that you would worsen, and in several months you will die. We sought a second opinion from a surgeon in Athens, and he confirms this fact. In fact, his opinion is that you will not make it till Christmas. I honestly do not know if I can absorb this fact. I cannot imagine life without you. Already it hurts me to see boys running with such ease and playing soccer. You can hardly walk now, and it becomes worse every day. You are now in a wheelchair and using a walker to move around the house.

I don't feel desperate, but I am aware of the pending emotions that lie ahead. They wait, looming over us until the moment you are gone – coming down the stairs and not finding you there; calling out your name and catching myself when I remember that there is no one there to respond; imagining what you would be like five, ten, or fifteen years from now; celebrating your birthday without you; and missing you terribly at Breanna's and Brett's weddings. All of these are deep emotions waiting to fall on us.

I know that you will be with Jesus, Travis. I am jealous of you. It will be more real than anything you have experienced here. You will *really* be there, Travis. Spiritual reality is more real than our reality. Oh, my son, you will see Him – our Lord. You will never know pain; you will know nothing but joy and peace. You will be free.

Surviving the Fires of Sorrow

I hurt for you now, but I long that if it is to happen, it will be soon. I do not want to see you suffer. You are so strong. Never complaining. Frustrated but not angry. I admire you deeply. You are an example to me, Travis. At the pond two days ago, you tried to throw a ball, but it never left your hand. You turned away and said, "Oh well, there are more important things in life anyways."

I plead with God to heal you. I remind him that your condition is no different from that of Jairus's daughter or the many other people whom Jesus healed. I ask God what is different with you that prevents His responding to you as He did to those fortunate ones. Healing would bring such glory to Him.

Travis, God has used you to break me. I am a broken man. Sometimes I wonder what would have become of me had none of this pain come my way this last year. He has purified me. There are no façades, no need for affirmation and applause. I will never be the same. Whatever happens, I will serve Jesus with all of my heart, soul, and strength. And I will do so limping.

Should He not heal you, I want to prepare you to meet Jesus in the time that is left, but I don't know how. It seems more that you are preparing me. You are prepared; I am not. We speak together about dying, but I am cautious not to say too much. I wish that you asked questions, but you say little about it. Perhaps you have no questions. God will help us prepare.

You are so tired today. You're on the couch right now sleeping next to me. The United States plays China today in the women's soccer finals. Viviane and her family will join us. It has been so special to watch you and Melanie together along with your other cousins, Sarah and Jason. It is hard on them. They love you so much.

I will close now and write you again later.

I love you,
Your Daddy

Chapter 25
Funeral Plans, Before Death

August 11

My Dear Travis,

    We are all together on Lake Lanier enjoying what seems to be our last vacation with you. We are on a houseboat provided by Lake Lanier and docked on a little island. The Make-a-Wish Foundation (a charitable organization that fulfills the wishes of terminally ill children) arranged this time for us. We are the only ones here. It is beautiful. The sun is just rising, and the water is so calm and clear. I tried to fish, but it is not the same without you.

    It's hard for us as a family to watch you die. There is hardly anything left in you. You can no longer move much, and your speech is almost gone. Your life is hanging by a thread, and we all know that you could be gone any time. Your mind is sharp, but you cannot express it. Still, you show no frustration or anger and continue to indicate that you are ready and eager to see Jesus.

Surviving the Fires of Sorrow

It's hard to imagine what life will be like without you, but we have to move on. I wonder what the pain of your absence will be like. Will it be similar to or different from the pain of seeing you suffer? Right now, I can see you. You're there. Soon you won't be. How long does it take the human spirit to get used to this? Will it always be painful?

Breanna told me yesterday that this is the best vacation she's ever had. She was steering the boat when she said this, and I wonder why she said it. I sense that she said it because we are not wallowing in your dying. Brett and Breanna will be the ones left with your mom and me. It will be important that we never hold back from them when we miss you. Going on this trip must be a way of communicating to her that we can still have fun, even in the worst of circumstances. I think that is why she said what she did. We need this time with you. Our house has been so busy – people passing through daily, like Brett and Breanna, always with a friend. It is rare for all of us to be in the same room together. We need to have this time with you alone, with no one else.

I told your mom last night that, on the one hand, I feel so free; on the other hand, I feel such pain for you. Yesterday, for the first time, I really felt so deeply sorry for you. We have to feed you. You can swallow only liquids now. You wet yourself at times. I remember feeding your mom to nurse her back to health, and here I find myself feeding you just to keep you going another few days. I really don't think you will be with us much longer.

Michael W. Smith called you last week. He heard about you from the Make-a-Wish Foundation, and he kindly took the time to call while on vacation in Hawaii. When I gave you the phone, you had no strength to talk. I took the phone from you, and Michael and I spoke for a few minutes. I explained that you have loved his music. I also shared briefly about what your mom has gone through and now what you are going through. It touched me that he called. I wonder if, years from now, he will remember this conversation.

I ask the Lord every day to whisper to your spirit words of comfort, reassurance, and encouragement. When I ask, you seem to indicate that you pray to Jesus often. I really wonder in what special ways the Lord speaks and reveals Himself to us as we die. You can't tell me, but I sense that something special is taking place between the two of you. Imagine interacting with the Lord before death. God must prepare us to meet with Him. I keep telling you that the moment you take your last breath, your spirit immediately leaves your body and enters the embrace of Jesus.

This reminds me of the poster I kept in my office in England. It was one of my favorite paintings. A man who has obviously died is greeted by Jesus with a huge bear hug. What a reunion, and what a special reception a *child* must receive. Jesus gave special attention to children while He was here, so I can imagine that He gives them VIP treatment there.

Pastor Harold Mangham visited last week and asked you what your favorite song was. "Big House," you said. The Audio Adrenaline song about the house that Jesus is preparing for you has given you words of hope. He shared this with the congregation last Sunday. Here are the words to that song:

I don't know where you eat your meals or where you talk on the telephone.
I don't know if you got a cook, a butler, or a maid.
I don't know if you got a yard with a hammock in the shade.
I don't know if you got a place where you can run and hide.
I don't know if you live with friends in whom you can confide.
I don't know if you live with a family, say a mom or dad.
I don't know if you feel love at all but I bet you wish you had.

Come, and go with me, to my Father's house.
Come, and go with me, to my Father's house.
It's a big, big house, with lots and lots of room.
A big, big table with lots and lots of food.
A big, big yard, where we can play football.
It's a big, big house.
It's my Father's house.

Surviving the Fires of Sorrow

All I know is it's a big ole house with room for everyone.
All I know it's got lots of land, where we can play and run.
All I know is that you're all alone, and I've got a family.
All I know is that you need love, so why not come with me?

Come, and go with me, to my Father's house.
Come, and go with me, to my Father's house.
It's a big, big house, with lots and lots of room.
A big, big table with lots and lots of food.
A big, big yard, where we can play football.
It's a big, big house.
It's my Father's house.[10]

I can't believe that I have had to make funeral plans for my twelve-year-old child. I told you about it yesterday. I visited the funeral home, chose a burial spot, and put a program together. It is so unnatural; yet, it is done with such routine and ease. David Harvey and I have met several times for lunch at a coffee shop. We meet to plan your funeral. We have papers out; we discuss the program, and we do it with the same attention and detail reserved for the planning of a Sunday worship service. Several times, tears welled up in my eyes. I looked at David and said, "David, can you believe that here we are planning the funeral for my son, and he is not even dead yet?"

David has been so compassionate, a true friend in a very difficult time.

I have begun a Bible study about passion in the book of Acts. I think that God will use this to prepare me to get back on the battle line. After Christ's death and resurrection, the church moved into action. It will be time for your mom and me to get back onto the battlefield. I'll go limping, but I'll go with a renewed love for Jesus. I am so indebted to Him. He has been so good to us. I don't want your death to keep me

---

[10] Audio Adrenaline, *Big House* (Franklin, Tenn.: The Forefront Communication Group, Inc., 1993).

from serving. I am making that commitment now, knowing that in the days of grief the wind will not be in my sails.

    I would like to read these letters to you today. I think it is time to do so, but there is no way you could absorb them.

I love you!

Chapter 26
Facing Death

I realize now that Travis will never be able to read these letters. Who are they for? I have written these for myself more than for Travis. I know that, but my hope in the beginning was that he would be able to read these years from now as a healed man. That does not seem to be the case; Travis will die. Death has been something which I have struggled to understand lately. Why is it that when we are faced with death, which happens to everyone, we become numb, confused, and lost?

August 17

Travis has been in a coma now for five days. The last time he responded to me was at Lake Lanier, I think, the last hour we were there. Even then, there was little response. I asked him a question, and he barely had strength to whisper his answer. His body has virtually shut down.

I just checked his temperature. The thermometer registered 106.5 degrees. I don't know if he is aware of himself or his surroundings. Right now, his mom and I are standing over him having just completed a discussion about dying. Our friend, David Harvey, came this morning with McDonald's breakfasts and commented that he wonders if the spirit leaves for Jesus before the body dies. That is what Elaine and I just debated.

In her own way, Elaine struggled to say, "No, I don't believe that. At the Cross, Jesus went through it all the way until the end, and so do we." Elaine has greater authority to speak of this than I. She was so close to death herself.

So many people drop by. Travis's friend and soccer partner, Philip, came by with his mom yesterday. He wept. I was so moved by it that I placed my arms around him and encouraged him to remember the commitment to Jesus that Travis had made. Apparently, he has taken this very hard. Other gestures of love and concern have moved me deeply. The sixth and seventh graders from Travis's school made more than two hundred cards. Also, they called for an early morning prayer meeting just for him, and more than one hundred children attended.

I wonder what death will be like for Travis. He will not know it as death like we do. To him, it will mean life - eternal life and the presence of Jesus.

Oh Travis, soon you will see Him face to face, the Holy God Himself. You will see the face that no living being can see while in the flesh, and you will live as you never knew life here.

But I wonder. What will it be like? God has kept the details from us, but the hope for it is so real and strong. The Scriptures have whetted our appetites, and when we refuse to live by the flesh, our longing for heaven runs deep in soul. "And the world is passing away along with its desires, but whoever does the will of God abides forever." (1 John 2:17).

I read Psalm 23 the other day. For the first time, I saw it as a psalm of death. Our Shepherd leads us to green pastures and calm waters. Only after death is our soul truly restored. As believers, we need not fear death. Jesus has conquered death and turned it into a catapult into eternity. Beyond that valley, where death hangs like a shadow, is a table prepared just for Travis. There is his home. He is ready for it. A feast awaits him, and the day will come when I will join him.

Taste the food for me, Travis, and save me a place!

Chapter 27
I'll See You There, Son

Sunday, August 22

This morning at 2:00, Travis joined the Lord Jesus. He was welcomed by a cheering crowd and escorted by the angels down a path to the very presence of his Lord and Savior. The Lord Jesus placed His arms around Travis, and together they laughed as Travis has never laughed before. They sat at a table and ate together, waited on by angels especially assigned to this task.

Elaine and I slept downstairs only several feet from Travis. For several nights, we slept that way, and the heavy breathing from his bed often kept me up. On many occasions, I knelt next to him and held him close. His body was warm, but that warmth was the only sign of life. There were many moments when the agonizing sounds of his breathing burdened me. I urged Travis to let go, telling him that Jesus was there waiting to take him.

"Go on, Travis," I would cheer. "Take His hand. He wants you."

Surviving the Fires of Sorrow

Well, last night the breathing stopped, and I jolted awake rushing to his side. He had just left us. My immediate reaction was to break out with the *Doxology*. Elaine joined me:

Praise God from whom all blessings flow;
Praise Him, all creatures here below;
Praise Him above, ye heavenly hosts;
Praise Father, Son, and Holy Ghost.

This was not planned but spontaneous. I was thankful to God for bringing this trial to an end and releasing my son into glory. The image of his lifeless body and later the somber scene of men in black carrying his body up the stairs I know will remain forever etched on the screen of my mind. Yet, that was no longer my son. It was only his casing, the container that held Travis Andrew Schultz for twelve wonderful years. His spirit is gone and so the body now no longer means anything to us. It must be discarded.

I don't understand why God took Travis so soon. Yet, the moment he died, I rushed to his side and felt a deep joy for him and, yes, also for me. Travis's death increases my longing to see Jesus, too. A reunion awaits us. It seems so clear right now. Oh Lord, don't let this clarity be lost. Keep away the fog and the mist that hide this reality.

Travis is with Jesus. We are left to miss him, yes, but to continue in service to our King.

My time – our time – here is so short. It will seem like only minutes when we, too, join those around that table. I can't wait, but I must.

Chapter 28
No Postcards from Heaven

Tuesday, August 24

Death confuses me. What happens after death confounds me. Why has God left out the details of life in heaven? I believe it all, and I believe firmly. My problem is not with doubt; it's with my perception of heaven. I know that the spirit goes immediately into God's presence. In Acts 7, Stephen cried out as a last prayer, "Lord Jesus, receive my spirit" (v. 59). Paul tells us that to be "…absent from the body is to be present with the Lord" (1 Cor. 5:8), and "to me, to live is Christ and to die is gain" (Phil. 1:21). So, heaven is better than here. It is a place where pain and death are absent and a place filled with unimaginable bliss. I believe with all of my heart and with every ounce of my being that Travis is consciously and actually in God's presence and loving it. It must be euphoric for him.

My problem these past days has not been believing it but imagining it. If I sent Travis to a favorite vacation spot knowing that he would have the time of his life, I could easily picture in my mind the factors that would contribute to his enjoyment: swimming, jet skiing, running in the sand, playing soccer, eating. But I can't conjure such specifics about heaven. I've never been there, and God has withheld many of the snapshots from us. The mailman brings no postcards with a return address marked "Heaven." Yet, what I do envision comes from pictures that the Bible gives us: a holy place, a lot of praise and music, angels, joy, the presence of God's saints, forgiveness, purity, and freedom from pain. Some people have said that Travis is playing soccer in heaven.

We tend to use earthly pleasures and try to project them heavenward, but it is far more than that. What exactly? I don't know. God hasn't told us. Why not? Two reasons, I think.

First, it is good for our faith not to know too much. Remember what Hebrews 11:1 says about faith? It is "being sure of what we hope for and certain of what we *do not see*." That seems like a contradiction, doesn't it? How in the world can we be certain about something that we can't see, especially in our scientific age? The Bible tells us that we anchor our certainty on the promises of God's Word. God tells us that it is worth the wait, and we take Him at His Word. He said it, and I believe it *even* though not all of it is clear to me. I love some of the words that John gives at the end of Revelation: "These words are trustworthy and true." He offers this assurance in Revelation 21:5. We believe what God tells us because He is trustworthy and true.

I also find great encouragement in 1 Peter 1:8-9. Peter urges us to put up with the grief of this life because one day we will receive what he calls the "goal of your faith." "Though you do not see him, you love him; and even though you do not see him now, you believe in him and are filled with an inexpressible and glorious joy, for you are receiving the goal of your faith, the salvation of your souls."

The moment that Travis died, he attained the goal of his faith – he got what God had promised him: the fulfillment of salvation. Although I don't see it all now, I believe it all by faith. Not knowing everything is good for my faith.

The second reason God withholds some of the details from us is that He knows what we would do with them. Had God told us exactly what heaven would be like, we would try to market it here on earth. Some things are best left to our imagination, and heaven is one of them. [I don't at all take seriously or believe the stories that have been written by those claiming to have been to heaven and returned. In one case, the account of a young boy who purportedly died, went to heaven, returned, and then wrote a book about it turned out to be a hoax made up by his father. By then, the publisher and the family had raked in millions of dollars. When Paul was taken to the *third heaven* in 2 Corinthians 12, he clearly expressed that God would not allow him to speak about what he saw in heaven. Paul tells us that he "was caught up to paradise and heard inexpressible things, *things that no one is permitted to tell*" (2 Cor.12:4). Clearly, man's propensity is to profit off heavenly experiences.]

Perhaps there is also a third reason and that is that heaven simply cannot be put into human terms. Reading the images portrayed in Revelation suggests that the writer, John, can use only similes to describe heaven. It is *like* this or that. "I saw what looked *like*..." There are no human words to describe something like heaven. Heaven is indescribable.

I know that Travis is better off. I know that he is free from his suffering. I know that he is full of joy that far surpasses what he ever experienced here. I strain to imagine what he is doing right now, but I come up short. The screen of my mind is filled with only a vague and blurry image. Meanwhile, I must go on and nurture my own relationship with Jesus. The death of my son will be an event, one of the trials that God will use to "develop perseverance" and make me "mature and complete," as James tells us (1:4). I must move on, but serving Jesus must consume me more than conjuring images of heaven. Someday I too, will know that "inexpressible and glorious joy" when I receive the "goal of my faith" (1 Peter 1:8).

Wednesday, August 25

Death is an appointment. Now that is a hard thing to swallow. "Just as man is destined to die once…" (Heb. 9:27). The moment Travis's spirit left his body, he made his appointment. And it was on time. Now that is something that is even harder to swallow. What this means is that Travis lived a full life.

Wait a minute! I thought that a full life meant living to a ripe old age of seventy-four or more years.

[As I now reflect on what I wrote back then in this journal entry, let me give an example of what I meant. The summer after Travis died, our family traveled to Indiana where we took part in a memorial service for Elaine's grandmother. She was one hundred and three years old. She lived nearly eight times longer than Travis, and I am sitting here suggesting that both of them lived a full life? I can easily accept that Elaine's grandmother lived a full life, but I find it much harder to accept that a twelve-year-old child lived the full extent of his life. However, I believe in the absolute sovereignty of God who does all things perfectly.]

Psalm 18:30 goes so far as to say, "As for God, *his way* is perfect." Because God is sovereign, and because God is in complete control of Travis's situation, I have to believe, with conviction, that Travis died when God planned for him to die. If Travis's death were premature, a severe puncture threatens our belief in God's sovereignty. Consider what Psalm 139:16 tells us: "All the days ordained for me were written in your book before one of them came to be." The script for Travis's life on earth included twelve years and ten months. No more. The span of life is sovereignly determined.

I am currently reading the book *Deadline* by Randy Alcorn. It tells of a man who dies and goes to heaven. His early moments of bliss in heaven take place with the angel who had been assigned to him throughout his life. At one moment, the man asks his angel if the car accident that took his life was meant to happen. Following is an excerpt of the dialogue between Finney, the believer, and his angel friend:

"Finney asked, 'Did I die early?'

"Zyor replied, 'You did not die early any more than if you had died at twenty-five or ninety-five. Whoever walks with God is immortal until his work on earth is done. For such a one, there are no accidents.'"[11]

If Travis did, in fact, live out his full life, I am never meant to imagine what he could have been had he lived. At least I am not meant to be consumed by what he would have been as a teenager, a college student, or a father because it was never meant to be for him. That was never part of his script. As much as I should not imagine what Elaine's grandmother would have been as a one hundred twenty-year-old woman, neither am I to imagine Travis as a fifteen-year-old boy. What I *am* permitted to imagine is what he is experiencing now – sheer bliss.

We had the viewing for Travis last night. More than four hundred people showed up. It was not Travis there in that coffin. It did not even look like him. What defines a person in life is not the shape of his body. I saw a shell of a person, a completely lifeless corpse. That fact struck me especially the moment Travis died. As I looked at his lifeless body, I knew that it was no longer him. He was gone. I reminded the many children who were in line to see Travis's shell that that body was not Travis. He, the *real* Travis, is with Jesus.

---

[11] Randy Alcorn, *Deadline* (Sisters, Ore.: Multnomah Books, 1994).

Chapter 29
As Free as a Butterfly

Friday, August 27

It has been five days now since Travis went to be with Jesus. 2 Corinthians 5 has given me great comfort since the pastor preached on it at the funeral. Travis left his tent to be clothed with a house built by God. He groaned terribly in his old body. It was a tent that was worn and ripped by the harsh wind that had slapped against him this past year. I find courage in this fact. Yet since yesterday, the day after the funeral, the pain has been so intense.

For the months that preceded Travis's death, I schemed strategically to abbreviate the grieving process. I really believed that I could move quickly and easily to the acceptance stage, but in these days, I have felt the heaviness of anger and denial. I keep the anger well contained, but it is there. How can you not experience denial when the son you loved so dearly and played with so often is no longer there?

Looking at his body in the coffin, I imagined him opening his eyes, looking at me, and saying, "It really did not happen, Daddy."

C.S. Lewis compares the death of his wife to the phantom pains of amputation. You feel the old leg there and can even wiggle your toes. Look, though, and the leg is gone. My mind is so accustomed to Travis that it refuses to accept the fact that he is gone. Twelve years and he became so much a part of my life. The daily "kick abouts" in the yard, the jokes, and the imaginative games are all running like a movie reel in my mind, but they are no longer occurring.

Many people write nice things, but nice things, even if they are true, do not fill the vacuum. Someone wrote, "I do praise God that Travis is in a much better place." Better place? For whom? Not for me! What parent, upon receiving a brand new baby, would say, "This child would be better off in heaven?" The heart of all parents cries out that the child is better off with them. God did not give us children and then take them away because they are better off with Him. True, because of Travis's suffering in the last months, he *is* better off in heaven. But my parental heart says that he would have been better off healthy and with me.

I gave Travis to God for God to do with his life what He wanted. That does not mean that I like what God has done. I don't like it, but I have chosen to accept it.

The funeral service was a rich experience. Oh yes, I did experience God's presence there. People said so many nice things about Travis. He really did have an impact on others. Brett cried often throughout the service, and I guess that this was good, but it hurt. Last night, Breanna wanted to visit the grave site. I cried there. Brett said, "Daddy, why did you come here if you are going to cry?" I told him that I needed to cry, but children do not understand this need.

Travis's stone reads, "He's not here. With Jesus in the big, big house." I chose this cemetery because I pass it often. And every time I see the grave, I want to be able to say, "This is where Travis is *not*."

Sunday, August 29

Today marks a week since Travis died. I'm sitting on our deck absorbing all that this fact means to us. The emotions and the pain can be so complex and at times mixed with very small doses of joy. In time, I assume that the joy of knowing where Travis is will begin to serve as a balm on the wounded soul.

I was just reflecting about the joy that Travis must be experiencing. What is frustrating, at least right now, is that I cannot share in his joy. Parents find great joy in watching their children perform and learn and grow. We cheer the goals, we praise them for their report cards, and we admire their creative and imaginative art. The joy we experience at such times comes in part by participating with them in what they accomplish. It is visible and tangible, something that I can know and respond to with my physical senses. Now, I can only experience Travis's joy by faith. At this time, while his death is still a tender wound, that joy by faith is not enough, but it will be eventually.

Breanna provided us with a good object lesson today. Some weeks ago, her aunt sent her a butterfly set. The instructions informed Breanna to place the cocoons in the box and then to wait. After two weeks, the cocoons burst to give birth to five beautiful butterflies. Their home for these past weeks had been a box, about one and a half feet square. Until today, this box was their world, the only world they knew. Today, Breanna ordained that these butterflies be set free. Perhaps having come from their cocoons, they thought that they were free. But they discovered a new freedom that involved a far larger world than they ever imagined, one filled with pleasures unknown to them in the confines of the "box" world. Perhaps, when Breanna first opened that box, they experienced fear and uncertainty. Once coaxed from their safe confine, several stumbled out afraid to test their wings. Guided by a slight breeze, however, the butterflies floated safely over the deck and knew that their wings were meant for the enjoyment of a new, much more gratifying freedom. We've not seen them since.

Travis lived the whole of his life in this earthly box. It was the only box he knew, and for twelve years it served as his home, but it was not the world that was meant to be his permanent home. God ordained that Travis be released from the small, cramped confines of this world to enter a new world. Until we are released from this world through death, none of us really knows how wonderful God's new home for us is. Travis was released to enjoy a new freedom, incomparable to what he understood earthly freedom to be. In fact, life here was meant to be only a rehearsal for the real play, which he is now enjoying.

I like the way Joseph Bayly handles the dilemma of longing for heaven without proof of its existence in his book *The Last Things We Talk About*. It is, I think, even better than my box analogy. He writes:

> If I were a twin in the womb, I doubt that I could prove the existence of earth to my mate. He would probably object that the idea of an earth beyond the womb was ridiculous, that the womb was the only earth we'd ever know. If I tried to explain that earthlings live in a greatly expanded environment and breathe air, he would only be more skeptical. After all, a fetus lives in water; who could imagine its being able to live in a universe of air? To him such a transition would seem impossible.
>
> It would take birth to prove the earthly existence to a fetus. A little pain, a dark tunnel, a gasp of air - and then the wide world! Green grass, laps, lakes, the ocean, horses, rainbows, walking, running, surfing, ice skating.[12]

Thank you, Joseph Bayly, for this picture. You had three children die, so you know the pain.

---

[12] Joseph Bayly, *The Last Things We Talk About* (Elgin, Ill.: David C. Cook, 1969), 116.

Chapter 30
Life Goes On

September 2

It was Brett's birthday yesterday. Someone was missing at this party. It's funny how small things enlarge the awareness of loss. Someone wanted to take our family picture the other day. I noticed that only four make up our family now. Elaine sets the table for our meal – four plates. We pile into the car. Only two children shuffle for seats now.

Then there is that empty room which is always painfully neat. No clothes to pick up. No ruffled, slept-in sheets to change. Eight hours later absolutely nothing has changed in that room. It is like walking into a photograph with every little trinket and toy exactly where it was the last time you were in the room.

I remember some years ago talking to a friend whose wife had died after a lengthy illness. I asked him what the hardest thing was about being alone. His answer? Coming home after work and finding the newspaper lying exactly where he had left it that morning.

There is certainly a strange stillness in death. How little we notice the normal, mundane activities of children until they are gone. I wonder how long it takes to get over this.

Breanna was baptized last Sunday at Toccoa Falls, just one week after Travis joined Jesus in the fulfillment of baptism. She gave a beautiful testimony that morning. I loved her deeply when I baptized her.

And Brett? Is it that I have not noticed him this past year? Has my attention and energy been so much on caring for Travis that I have not observed how handsome and polite Brett is? I remarked to Elaine how Brett is so much like Travis, always laughing, very polite and caring, and feathers never ruffled. I am careful not to project my feelings for Travis on Brett because I do love him dearly. I pray for him now that he would be what we named him – "God is my Judge." We pray that God would be his measure, the standard by which he lives his life.

Sunday, September 5

Words from Pastor Les's message at the funeral keep bouncing off the walls of my mind. "Travis was not sacrificed so people would come to Jesus. Jesus was that sacrifice. Travis was merely an example of someone who gave his life to serve God."

People are coming to Jesus because of Travis. Many others make deeper commitments. Some of them are committing themselves to be missionaries. Last Wednesday, Elaine and I attended the weekly prayer meeting. A missionary stood up to share how, at a service in North Carolina, they told of the testimony of Travis. He said that many people came forward to commit their lives to serve Jesus. Later, one father called the missionary and related that during the invitation the father's seven-year-old son had said, "Daddy, I want to go up to the front because I want to take Travis's place as a missionary."

We also heard of an evangelist in South America who related the story of Travis and called upon everyone there to give their lives to Jesus as Travis had done. The altar, we are told, was full. Another man shared Jesus with a lady on an airplane. He felt led to explain to her the events surrounding the funeral and the impact that Travis had had on so many people. The lady responded by giving her life to the Lord Jesus Christ.

My sister commented that at least it is good to see some of the reasons why Travis was taken. Maybe I was a bit strong, but I responded that these were not God's reasons for taking my son; rather, they were the results of my son's death.

Elaine and I have mixed feelings when we hear such stories. Others praise God much more easily than we do. I do praise God, but it is not the sort of praise that erases the pain. We marvel at what God is doing, but Travis is still our precious son who suffered and died. I cannot really say that he was taken from us because we gave him to the Lord Jesus. That which we are witnessing and marveling at is what God will do with what we place on the altar. If we have honestly given our children to Him, we have no right to argue with what He does with that sacrifice. Travis was God's to do with as He wanted. This is what God chose, and we can only stand back and painfully and humbly thank Him that He is receiving the glory for it.

When we dedicate our children to God and then argue with Him when He does something of which we don't approve, it is hypocrisy. Baby dedication will never be the same for me. If I ever officiate at a dedication, I will urge the parents to consider seriously what they are saying. Like Jonah, we must be able to say, "What I have vowed I will make good" (Jonah 2:9).

I took Breanna and Brett to the water park yesterday, a day full of laughter, splashes, and sheer fun. Yes, we can have fun. There is certainly no despair. The awareness of loss and a slight pressure of heaviness on my heart is there, but it does not burden me. I am overwhelmed by the peace of God, and yes, it does certainly surpass all understanding.

September 12

My view of God has shifted drastically these past few months. God is no longer convenient. When life seemed easy, I had control, and God was One to turn to at designated moments. Now that I need Him, He frightens me. He has become a mystery, no longer the pal to whom I could turn to at my convenience. My view of God needed to change. It is funny how songs about God, particularly contemporary ones, seem so flippant. References to God intermingled with the la-di-da beats just don't move me anymore.

Who is this God who gives life and directs that life, even choosing to snuff it out with no warning or explanation? Who is this God who seems silent when well-intentioned elders surround a dying twelve-year-old boy to anoint him with oil? Who is this God who provides supernatural peace to sustain us through this loss?

In his book *A Grief Observed*, C. S. Lewis faced a vastly different God following the death of his wife than he knew before her death. Wondering if God is a Cosmic Sadist, Lewis confesses:

> Not that I am (I think) in much danger of ceasing to believe in God. The real danger is of coming to believe such dreadful things about him. The conclusion I dread is not 'So there is no God after all,' but 'So this is what God's really like.'[13]

This is the view of God that I now have. "So this is what God is really like." My recent crisis has revealed that all along I have been looking at God from the wrong mountain. I am just now beginning to know Him. "'For my thoughts are not your thoughts, neither are your ways my ways,' declares the Lord" (Isa. 55:8). Yet, Hosea 14:9 tells me that, nevertheless, "The ways of the Lord are right."

---

[13] C.S. Lewis, *A Grief Observed* (New York: Seabury, 1963), 5.

Chapter 31
Motivation to Move On

October 30

I am seated on a lawn chair overlooking two beautiful ponds. One is adjacent to me, covered with lilies, and a larger one is one hundred yards in front of me with a boardwalk extending a third of the way into it. The occasional splash of a certain fish in the pond next to me has interrupted what has turned out to be two necessary hours of solitude. Elaine and I are in South Georgia to be involved in a local church tonight and tomorrow morning. Elaine is not yet back from speaking at a ladies' luncheon.

What do I make of this woman? Ten months ago, she scrambled to put two words together, and now she is speaking publicly. The sentences are not always grammatically structured, and her range of words is still limited, but the woman has courage.

I remember writing a plea to God in my journal many months ago. "Lord," I said, "if you take Travis to be with you, at least give Elaine full recovery." Sometimes God works in inches, not in the more welcome miles. I have been deeply encouraged by her progress though. Today's five-hour trip was filled with good conversation. She has a way to go, but she will get there. Her reading is developing; her writing is still in the early stages.

I fear solitude, but I still need it. Stillness offers me uninterrupted time to hear God speak to my restless heart. I fight anxiety, particularly in new settings. This is my second week in a row away from home. Last weekend, all four of us flew to Milwaukee. I prefer the cocoon environment of Toccoa, but as God dealt with Moses, He heals a man and restores him in isolation only for a season. A moment comes when it is time to move out and brave the new winds. Service to Jesus demands it.

I wonder if I have changed much this last year. Others must see a change. How can a man go through so much and not change? I don't think that I laugh much. In fact, when I laugh, I feel guilty – as though it is unfair to the process of grief. Sorrow can become a trap to the mourner.

Someone told Elaine the other day that I should smile more.

"He looks good when he smiles."

Well, frankly, I haven't had much to smile about recently. This has been a year-and-a-half-long ordeal for me, and the effect upon my character has been deep.

I just reviewed Acts 6 for devotions this morning. Just before his death, Stephen, consumed by God, reviews the history of God's relationship with His people. Abraham's story reveals the God of Promises. The promise sealed with a covenant meant most when Abraham had nothing: no heir, no inheritance, and no land. God's promises mean the most to us when nothing seems evident.

Joseph's story reveals the God of Purpose. All of the turmoil in Joseph's life was designed for a purpose. This fact speaks to me. Moses's story, that of a weak man serving a weak nation, reveals the God of Power. "When I am weak, then I am strong" (2 Cor. 12:10).

This view of God was available to Stephen at his death because it was the view that he possessed during his life. How we die will be determined by how we lived.

I need to get ready now to preach at the morning service. "O Lord, help me to be motivated. Why is it so hard?"

November 16

This week it is Travis's birthday. He was born on November 19, 1986. Someone kindly and graciously told us yesterday at church that they would be praying as we move toward that date. Elaine and I discussed this and concluded that it is not the big days (birthdays, Thanksgiving, and Christmas) that will be hard but the small, unexpected moments like a passing comment by someone about Travis. For example, a letter from friends in England referred to their son's bike, which once belonged to Travis. This innocent and inadvertent comment brought to the surface a flood of emotions and memories. At other times, the simple mention of his name is enough to bring about a choked response. Last week, I took the children to school and returned feeling quite encouraged. The moment I pulled into our driveway, a memory passed quickly through my mind of Travis playing with his remote control car in the driveway. I think that we will handle the big days well. With them, we can easily brace ourselves and adjust with plans and distractions, but we have no way to prepare for the unexpected.

I'm actually on a plane right now returning to Atlanta from Baltimore. I was there to participate in a missionary conference, this time without Elaine. It has been a rich weekend, filled with opportunities to speak and encourage others through my testimony and messages from God's Word. Yet, I am the one who was really encouraged. The show of love and expressions of support have been like a flood of water covering parched land. Many people have come to me sharing how God has given them victory over deep trials.

For example, one man named Allen approached me after the service and introduced himself by saying, "I lost my wife and two children in a car accident." *God, forgive me for thinking I am the only one who suffers*, I thought.

Our world is a hard one. Stories abound of courageous men and women who have overcome. God's promises are meant to keep and sustain us in our moments of crisis. They encourage us in times of peace, but they carry us in our trials. This is what gives me motivation to move on.

Chapter 32
Thankfulness for the Grace of Endurance

November 25 – Thanksgiving Day

It is Thanksgiving today, a wet and rather dreary day. We all woke up quite cheery, and I even took time to read a book to Breanna about the Mayflower. Elaine's parents are visiting, and our time with them has been pleasant. Hans, my friend from Holland, has also come to visit. When Travis was first diagnosed, Hans immediately came across the ocean to visit and encourage us.

Elaine and I noted this morning that today does not feel much like Thanksgiving. We did not really make much of Thanksgiving during our six years in England. Thanksgiving is not a hard holiday to get through in light of Travis's absence. Last night before bed, however, I suddenly became overwhelmed by a dark cloud of grief. Like an unexpected bolt of lightning on what seemed like an otherwise clear and calm day, a sudden memory struck at my heart.

Hans and I visited the graveside. I have not visited much – probably once every two weeks. I had convinced myself that I have not needed to go. *After all, he is not there*, I tell myself. You want me to be honest? I avoid the place. I stand over that piece of green plot now defined as the burial ground for my son. For as long as we live and as long as creation remains undisturbed, that area, ten feet by eight feet, belongs to us. We bought that land. Our first and only real estate is property purchased to dispose of the body of our son – not to build a house and not to invest money, but to bury Travis. I stand over that ground and think, *the body of my son is six feet under*. I have accepted his death, but I have denied myself some of the necessary emotions of grief.

What do I have to be thankful for today? The Thanksgiving Day lists are usually upbeat and festive. Today, the list is brief, and the pen is dipped in the ink of pain. Really, I have only one thing for which I am thankful today. I am thankful for the grace of endurance. Like Paul, I cling to the thought, "If we endure, we shall reign with Him" (2 Tim. 2:12).

December 5 – The Ring

The last thing I did after Travis died was to remove his ring from his finger. We had talked about what to do with that ring, and he had given clear instructions. I was not to remove it from his finger until *after* he was gone. One day, I walked into the room where Travis was lying on the couch. By this time he was very disabled, limited to the use of only his hands and his arms. He was staring at his ring and rubbing each of the letters engraved on the ring. The letters were *WWJD* (What Would Jesus Do). I knew at that moment that Travis must have been thinking about Jesus.

The story of this ring goes back to the week before he was diagnosed. He had been in school only a couple of weeks and was impressed by how many students at the middle school wore bracelets or rings with the marking WWJD. He pleaded with me to go to the Christian bookstore so that he could buy the ring. Shortly after he was diagnosed, I bought it for him. That ring, or more importantly that theme, served one important purpose during the months of his illness. "What Would Jesus Do?" was an important question to Travis and one that, I believe, gave him courage during the harder months. We know what Jesus did; He suffered. "He endured the cross, scorning its shame" (Heb. 12:2). He remains our model for how to handle suffering. I wonder if that was what Travis was thinking as he stared at the ring. What would Jesus do? He endured! He trusted! He did not complain!

Travis and I made an agreement about the ring. I am to give it to Brett when he turns twelve. I plan to engrave on the inside of the ring, "Brett, Love Travis – 12." Until that day, this ring will remain at the end of a necklace around my neck. [Today, Brett wears that ring, and when asked about it, he eagerly explains how he received it.]

After all of the years that I invested in Travis, my energy and time are now directed toward Breanna and Brett. I cannot and will not allow my grief for Travis's death to overshadow my love for them. Brett brings me such joy. At six, he is already gentle and obedient like his brother was, but he is his own person. Breanna, now ten, is a precious jewel. Rarely a moment goes by that I do not look at her with deep love. Her laughter, strength, and high standards have given all of us the courage to move on. Both of these children will serve God more deeply because of their loss.

December 23 – Facing Christmas

Facing Christmas is not easy for those who have suffered loss. The burden of loss weighs so much more heavily than the usual desire to be festive. People who have lost a loved one often dread this season because their experience and mood doesn't seem to match the festive atmosphere.

I have concluded that it does not have to be this way. In fact, the experience of loss and pain can actually reinforce and deepen the whole Christmas theme. You see, beyond the tinsel and behind the glitter and lights of Christmas is a somber message: God became man to suffer and die for mankind. The child born in that stable was born under horrible circumstances. He was born into a world of brokenness, sin, and separation from God. That child was born with one purpose and that was one day to finish on a cross. The path from infancy through childhood and adolescence to the Cross would be paved with pain and sacrifice.

I have recently noticed a new Christmas ornament for the Christmas tree. It is a long spike, a reminder at Christmas of the nail driven into the hands and feet of the One born in a stable and laid in a manger. The sweet, tender fingers of that child would later tighten in pain under the agony caused by that spike. Those small, perfect, unused feet would later hold the weight of a body weakened by the torture of dangling helplessly on a cross.

A person who is suffering loss should not feel out of place at Christmas. This core message of Christmas is the theme of my heart right now: death, loss, pain, sadness mingled with joy, and gratitude to God. At Christmas, we celebrate a mixed barrel. God became man to suffer, and die, but then to rise again that we might each live. The mood might be somber this Christmas, but it matches the mood of the first Christmas. I will not dread this first Christmas without Travis. Rather, I plan to face it and allow its deep, mysterious message to serve as a soothing balm to my yet tender wounds. There is no better time of the year to allow God to begin mending my broken heart.

In the Jewish celebration of Passover, each person partakes from a bowl of bitter herbs. A child asks why they eat the herbs, and the father explains that it is to remember the bitter years of captivity and the trials of the Exodus. While eating bitter herbs at Christmas might not be our custom, we should not forget that the context of Christ's birth was a bitter one. He was born into a world pinned under the bondage of sin and enveloped in darkness. I want to be somber this Christmas. I want to allow God's Spirit to minister the full message of Christmas on the soil of my torn soul. The seed planted will produce a rich harvest of praise for the greatest Gift of God.

Earlier this month, I read the following comforting words from Spurgeon's *Morning and Evening*: "Here, the sense of joy may come and go, but this will one day be changed gloriously. If to die is to enter into uninterrupted communion with Jesus, then death is indeed gain and the black drop is swallowed up in a sea of victory."[14]

---

[14] Spurgeon, *Morning and Evening*, Dec. 10.

Part 3

Brett and Us Since

Chapter 33
A Movie, Breanna, and It's Time for a Change

Summer 2018

I met the man in a cavernous lobby with people milling around waiting for the next session. It was May of 2005, and the man had been one of our pastors the year of Travis's illness. Since 2001, Elaine and I had been serving at a large church north of Milwaukee, and we were both attending our annual denominational conference. Pastor Harold Mangham reached out his hand to greet me, and both of us moved closer to avoid the bumps of people milling around us like a school of fish swimming past pieces of coral.

"Mitch." Both his firm grip and gentle eyes reminded me of his comforting words each Sunday at the close of many painful worship services during that hard year in Toccoa, GA. Back then, Pastor Harold would single me out of the crowd and come my way to spend a few minutes to see how I was doing. "I was looking for you and am glad we bumped into each other," he now said.

Eager to hear why the pastor had me on his mind during this busy conference, I leaned in fully attentive. He began to explain. "Next week, I'm starting what will likely be a yearlong interim work at one of our churches in Franklin, NC." I did not have to wonder long why he felt the need to single me out of the crowd to tell me this. "I've been thinking that you and Elaine would be the perfect couple to lead this hurting church."

I was overwhelmed. Harold did not know that for about six months I'd been praying for a possible change, sensing in my heart that I might be ready to take on a lead role in a church. This excited me. Seeing that people were leaving the lobby for the next session, I looked at Harold and tried to sound calm. "Tell you what, Pastor. This sounds really interesting, but when you're ready, contact me about this. I will not reach out to you, but you reach out to me." Or, I might have jokingly said, "Have your people call my people, and let's talk."

Nine months later the call came, not from him but from the superintendent of that district. My resumé was sent, and a month later I snuck to my church office for what turned out to be an hour-and-a-half long phone interview with that church board. The building was dark except for my office. When the interview was over, I leaned back, sighed, and then I laughed. I realized how ridiculous it was to sneak around like this to make sure no one saw me and to assume that if they did they would know exactly what I was doing. I leaned forward to straighten out a couple papers where I'd jotted some notes and smiled again. The interview went well, and I had this deep gut feeling, the kind that always makes me think this is where God confirms things with us. I got up, turned the light off and laughed again when I realized I had turned all the other lights off in the building and stood in complete darkness.

A couple weeks later, our daughter Breanna knocked on our bedroom door. It was late, and the four of us had just returned from seeing the movie <u>End of the Spear</u> which is about the martyrdom of

Jim Elliot by the Auca Indians in South America. Breanna, now seventeen and having matured past those harrowing early teen years of giving little attention to her parents, now seemed to want to include us in her life. She wanted to tell us something, so Elaine and I sat on the bed. Leaning her one shoulder against the wall, what came out of her heart through her lips surprised us. To this point, we had not told Breanna or Brett about a possible change. Yet, God must have been telling her something.

"I don't know," she stumbled through words grappling with how to begin, "but it's just, like, I don't know. Seeing that movie tonight really made me want to possibly talk to you guys about making a change." Without making it too obvious, Elaine and I made subtle eye contact, and I reached over to grab her hand to give it a squeeze.

I stood up and asked Breanna to sit down next to her mom. This time, I was standing. We then explained to her all that had transpired in the last months, and all she could says was, "Wow! Really? I wasn't really that serious about it."

Two weeks later, Elaine, Breanna and I took a trip south to Franklin, NC for a weekend of interviews and for me to preach that Sunday. Brett stayed home with some friends. That Saturday, the call and concern seemed routine. "Brett's been throwing up a lot," the host where he was staying explained.

"Well, just keep us posted," I said totally unconcerned. She did, and twice more she called to tell us he was not getting any better. A severe strain of a flu bug had been running rampant in the area, so we simply assumed he was its next victim. Four days later, I was back in Milwaukee having accepted the call to serve as the next senior pastor at the First Alliance Church in Franklin, NC. We would move that summer, only four months away. The excitement of this move quickly diminished, taking a back seat to Brett's continuing struggle with stomach pains and persistent throwing up.

The rest of that story unfolds in the form of a series of journal notes and several letters I wrote to Brett in the weeks that followed.

Chapter 34
Not Again! - Not You, Brett!

April 13, 2006

My Boy, Brett.

I have only known five children with cancer, and two of them are mine. Hearing that your child has cancer is something you cannot run from. Neither can you ignore it. You can't give it to someone else.

It's mine.

I own this.

Cancer. *Your son has cancer.* They are words that pierce and paralyze.

Again!

You have cancer!

Surviving the Fires of Sorrow

I am sitting next to you right now on this second day of your trial. The doctor came in yesterday to tell us the results of the biopsy following your surgery to remove a tennis ball-sized tumor from your abdomen. Now we know why you were sick all these weeks and why you lost nearly twenty pounds, a thin boy to begin with but now far thinner.

Burkitt's Lymphoma.

This is no lightweight cancer. We don't know the stage yet. The oncologist said he would call us in the next couple days to tell us.

I'm not really sure how you took the news that we are moving. You seem to be accepting it. However, in Dr. Tick's office at our last visit, he suggested that your stomach pains and throwing up was due to the emotional reaction to moving. "It happens to many kids his age," he argued. This angered me. I knew you might be struggling, but this is not you. You're not like that. You take things in stride for the most part, resilient and strong. Hey, look what you had to go through. Your mom's sickness. Travis dying. I know you're strong. There is no way this is emotional.

Some are suggesting that this is happening for spiritual reasons because we are moving. People are so quick to make connections. Is the devil trying to keep us from moving, or is this the Lord? How can we ever know? It's too big for me. I told my dad earlier today that I feel either chosen or targeted. How do you tell the difference? Gramps suggested it might be both.

It's strange that you are the same age as Travis, and you, too, have cancer. Travis never reached 13. Will you? Why does that question torment me right now? I shrug it off quickly before it makes its way past the mind to settle in my heart. Three weeks ago when you were really sick, I began to wonder if this was more serious, something far more than a stomach bug or an emotional reaction to moving as the doctor insisted.

You're so dear to me, Brett. Since losing Travis, you and I have been so close. I'm not sure what to do with this pain. We're told that Burkitt's is a serious cancer, very rare in the USA. Only around 200 a year are diagnosed. It's mostly diagnosed in Africa and was discovered by a Dr. Burkitt. We're being told it's a treatable cancer, but of course that depends on the stage. The best case scenario, we are told, is that you have a 90-95% chance of surviving. Worst case: 40-45%. Weird to give you a number like this. You're my son, not a statistic.

About ten people were in the room when the doctor and several interns entered. He did not waste time telling us it was cancer. Many broke down and cried, and the room was somber, painfully so. People lingered, shocked as we were, too shocked to comfort us. I remembered feeling annoyed.

When Breanna found out after your surgery that this was cancer, she came to see you at the hospital. After she showed up, I asked everyone to leave the room. We were supposed to go to Florida on vacation next week, but I don't think that will happen. Breanna leaned down next to you and said, "Thanks for ruining our vacation, Brett." I knew she was joking and trying to lift what was obviously a heavy cloud. You immediately laughed, and we joined in. That one moment with teasing words set the trajectory of how we will face this. Not necessarily with humor but with perspective. Our family is already close from all we've gone through, and I know we can withstand this. But, I have to be honest, Brett. Despite the healing we have experienced these past five years in this wonderful church, I feel weaker than I did when Travis was diagnosed."

I remember looking at you and Breanna together on that bed, still laughing and joking, and thinking, "Will she be my only child?"

I love you,
Dad

Surviving the Fires of Sorrow

My Dear Boy,

I was supposed to speak at the Good Friday service today. My text was to be from Isaiah 53:10. "It pleased the Lord to strike him." Strange verse isn't it? God actually delighted in His Son's pain? I was going to ask this question: Why did God desire to crush His Son? As your father, I do everything possible to keep you from hurting. Yet, here God wants to see His Son hurt. My message would have gone on to explain that it was Christ's obedience and the outcome of His suffering that pleased His Father. Christ's sacrifice would be a gift offering to His Father. I obviously ended up not giving that talk, but as I watch you suffer, this passage comforts me.

Yesterday was a raw day for me, Brett. I don't want this. This time I would love to give this to someone else if I could, but there is no one to give it to. But I am wrong. There is One to whom I can give this burden, not for Him to take it from me but to share it with me. Yesterday I read Oswald Chambers's explanation on Psalm 55:22 where he says that we must "cast our burden on the Lord. There are some burdens placed on us by God which he does not intend to lift off. God wants us to roll them back on him." Didn't Jesus tell us that He would take the burden from us? "My yoke is easy and my burden is light" (Matthew 11:30). Chambers continues capturing this thought like this: "The burden God places on us squeezes the grapes in our lives and produces the wine…[15]"

After the oncologist left the room where we discussed treatment options, Mom broke down. She had not had a chance to do this until now. How much more can this amazing woman take? I prayed hard for her. *Oh Jesus, don't do this to her. Don't take her only boy left away from her.* I think often, more recently than I did back then, that Mom hardly had time to grieve Travis's death. The only energy she had was to cope with her own losses. A mother unable to grieve the dying of her son for ten months! Mom and I prayed together now. Our words anointed with

---

[15] Oswald Chambers, *My Utmost for His Highest*, rev.ed. (Nashville: Thomas Nelson, 1992), April 13 and 14.

tears turned this pain, your pain, into a pledge to Jesus. We will trust Him, again. We prayed that somehow He would use us to be examples to others in this hospital and beyond. I find my desire for this is less than it was with Travis. That pain was so fresh, so new. Committing you and your situation to Jesus is harder this time around, like a veteran soldier, glowing in his past successes, asked to go into the battlefield again. But now he's tired. Too tired to fight and too tired to face loss again.

I love you,
Dad

My Dear Boy,

I've been weeping a lot today. People look at me, worried. I can tell. They don't say it, but the concern shows in their faces. Some expressed that we were allowing the mood in the room to be too solemn while others were visiting. I reprimanded a friend from church for saying this, reminding her that when the doctor told us you had cancer, it was the reaction of others in the room that created this mood. Mom and I decided to protect you from others for the next couple days and to give us space too. I put a note on the door asking people to knock, and we would come to open the door for them. We ignored several knocks.

We were told we would receive the preliminary report on the bone marrow biopsy today some time, but it's already five in the afternoon and no word. I am anxious. These are the hardest moments. This is like opening an old wound I thought had long ago scarred. If the cancer is in the bone marrow, you will have the worst kind of Burkitt's Lymphoma. I am preparing for that. It makes no difference to hope for the best. So, I just prepare for the worst. What else can I do? So many are praying for you. The church in Franklin, I am told, is fasting today. A group from church here told me they would fast everyday till this storm passes. I feel guilty, Brett, that I am expecting the worst when so many are praying for a good outcome. Perhaps it's because I was tossed so far into the sea of disappointment that I would rather stand on the shore of realism this time around.

Strange how much has happened these past few weeks. Three weeks ago I stood before the church family announcing that we would be moving to a new ministry. I explained to them that here we had experienced healing. We came here to recover, and we leave restored. This church has been amazing. They wept with us in the news that we were leaving.

Now this!

What do you do with what seemed like such clear direction from the Lord? From the day we were asked to consider this new position in North Carolina, I told the Lord that as long as the doors remained opened, I would keep walking through them. Now this door seems shut, and we find ourselves standing in a dark corridor unsure where the door even is. I plan on calling the elders in Franklin to ask them to release us from this commitment and call. There is no way I am going to do this with what you are going through. Last night, the elders here in Mequon met and voted to lay aside my resignation until we have clearer direction. They want us to stay here as long as we need to, even long term if it comes down to that.

Mom and I teased each other over a blanket draped over our coach. Here's what happened. There is a quote you might have heard: "When God closes a door, He always opens a window." I don't even know what this means. I told Mom, "So what are we supposed to do, jump out of that window?" And then I came up with my own variation to that expression, promising to one day have it woven into a new blanket. "When God closes a door, my fingers get slammed." To that Mom retorted, "When God closes the door, it's dark, cold, and lonely. So dark, we don't see where that window is."

God is more a mystery to me now than He's ever been! But, oh how I love Him and trust Him still.

I love you,
Dad

My Dear Boy,

Last night we received good news. You have no cancer in the bone. This means this is not stage four cancer, which leaves either stage three or maybe two. I'd prefer stage one, but we were told that would not be the case. Who came up with these stages anyway? Men wearing white coats who love chalkboards, no doubt.

This time only the four of us were in the room when the doctor came in to present this news. You and Breanna were watching a movie together. I went home feeling so good. What a relief! I'll just be honest with you, but this news was really the difference between knowing if you would live or if you would die. Blunt, isn't it? For days I lived with the agony, the real prospect of seeing another son die. Stage four is bad! Real bad! Just like I did when Travis was diagnosed, I dug in on the internet and took in all I could about your cancer. It forced me to accept that you could die. So when I looked last week at Burkitt's Lymphoma, I found that the stages really matter. Stage two is good, well if cancer can be good. Stage three is okay, most survive. Stage four: bad, really bad. Few survive. So you can see how knowing that the cancer is not in your bone marrow is really good news. It moves your situation from really bad, to *this is okay, we will beat it*. But we have more tests to go through to find out the extent of your cancer, and meanwhile you will have to undergo chemo treatment. We should know in a couple days.

I love you,
Dad

My Dear Boy,

I phoned our good friend, Eleri, in England today. She wept. She was a stalwart friend of ours when Mom was sick. I think you remember her. She is baffled that we are asked to go through so much but more baffled that we are taking it the way we are. I'm not sure I have an option to take it any other way. When you think about it, what choice does anyone have when hit with bad news like this? I also look at you and see how you are taking it, and how can I be mad? We really have two options when faced with a crisis: give up or keep going. Not sure what giving up means. I have to admit, though, I am struggling to accept this as well as I did with Travis's situation. With him, I remember easily telling people that God was in this, that I trusted Him, and that we would be okay. Maybe I am just tired; maybe I don't possess the same freshness and innocence in my faith. I'm not sure. I fight off anger toward God that I did not feel when your brother was sick.

I love you,
Dad

My Dear Boy,

I spoke to Harold, the interim pastor in Franklin. He's the one that first connected me with this church. We are supposed to leave in just two months, but it looks like we will wait until some time in August or September. They are willing to wait for us. Amazing! Part of me wishes they would tell me, "Thank you, but no thanks." I'd prefer to just stay here, but I guess we need to keep moving. I feel sorry for Harold. He's close to 80, and I know he just wants to retire and go back to Florida. Now he has to hang on for a couple more months or more. I told him we will know more once we get some tests back to see if the cancer shows up in other nodes. That will be the difference between stage two and three.

I'm not sure you knew this. Pastor Bill was supposed to take a four month sabbatical this summer, and I was going to preach the entire time he was gone. Several months ago, when we knew we'd be candidating in Franklin (long before we knew of your cancer), we called Pastor Bill and asked if he could come over to our house. He looked nervous standing on our porch, and we asked him to come in. We broke the news to him, and he took it hard. I don't think it was because it would affect his sabbatical alone but also because he was losing me as the associate pastor. This has been such a great place for us. It has been good for you and Breanna and a great place for our family to heal. Anyways, he's getting used to the idea and decided to put off his sabbatical until next year. It strikes me that this is affecting a lot of people, not just our family. I guess this is what Paul meant when he said in 1 Cor. 12:26, "If one member suffers, all suffer together; if one member is honored, all rejoice together."

I love you,
Dad

My Dear Boy,

I bumped into my friend Steve in the church kitchen today. His son Brad was in a car accident in March and has some serious physical and some neurological challenges. After he gave me an update, I told him for the first time about what you're going through. It seemed strange to hear myself tell someone that my twelve year old has cancer. Every time I tell people, it sounds as though I am hearing it for the first time. At least I feel the lump in my throat and that ache in my stomach each time. How many times do you have to tell a hard story before it becomes believable or stops hurting so much?

I think about what is normal. What *is* normal anymore? Normal for me, for us, is past tense. Normal marriage. Normal home. Healthy people, healthy wife, three healthy children. That is normal. *This* is not normal. Now the new normal will be your mom continuing to struggle through her disabilities, living with the loss of one son, and hopefully living with the story of another son who's survived cancer. I guess normal has stages like cancer has stages. And as with cancer, you adjust to these normals like turning a dial to find the right output on a machine. You get to normal by adjusting the dial of your life to where the pain is bearable and you hope it just stays like that or gets better. Normal and acceptance are synonyms, I think. To fight and reject pain is abnormal. You don't win, so you give in to it. You make room for the pain in your life and learn to live with it.

Surviving the Fires of Sorrow

As a pastor, Brett, I see a lot of people face hardship, and they can't cope. They don't adjust the dial, and it breaks them. Eventually they either give up, leave family, leave church, live with bitterness and anger, or they give in, and a sweet thing happens. Their lives, now shaped by the trial, makes them useful people in the hands of Jesus. I'll share this with you and hope it helps you someday. With each trial (Mom's cancer, Travis's cancer and with this) there was a very specific point of surrender. With Mom, it was when she was having surgery. The point of surrender came immediately. With Travis, it took a bit longer. I resisted several weeks until, in our back yard, I gave in to Jesus and told Him He had permission to do what He wanted. With you, well I'll admit, I am still in process. But I know what I need to do. The decision I make with this will determine the kind of person I will be years from now. The picture of a crotchety old man, bitter at life and hard to be around, doesn't appeal to me. I'd rather be sweetened by this trial, and I am working at giving this over to Jesus. But it's harder than it was for Mom and Travis's trials. I think it is because this is the third time it's happening to us.

I love you,
Dad

My Dear Boy,
We were supposed to go to Disney in Florida next week. Of course, now we can't.

I love you,
Dad

My Dear Boy,
Today is Easter Sunday. I thought a lot today about how the resurrection of Jesus extends hope to every trial. The resurrection promises relief. Had Jesus not died and risen from the dead, we would be without hope.

I slept in late this morning. I was supposed to give an update on your situation before Pastor Bill's sermon, but I came in late. This was the only reason I was going to go to church today. I did end up staying, and it was so hard to leave. Everyone wanted to talk. People came from every direction to give me a hug and ask how you were doing. Some gave a word of encouragement or offered to pray. It was amazing. This is the body of Christ at work. We have so many good friends here, and it will be hard to leave, especially with all this going on.

This afternoon someone came with a signed card with 200 signatures of well wishers. I took the card to you at the hospital, and I think it really encouraged you. I am not sure you totally understand what is going on. My heart aches for you. I know the idea of moving has been hard on you. You are a sensitive boy, so kind and caring, funny and deep. I love those moments where I lie in bed with you and tell you stories. When I leave, you urge me to stay by using a little guilt. "Come on, Dad. Someday you will look back and say, 'I should have spent more time with my boy.' Don't live with regret, Dad. Stay longer." We always laugh, and you do that often, even when I do stay with you for a long time. Now I don't want to leave your side at all.

I know this will impact you for life. How can anyone be the same after experiencing what you are going through and have gone through? I pray a lot that you won't have to suffer through this. They are talking to us about the kind of chemo treatment you will need, and I ache, picturing you weakening (you're already weak) and losing your hair.

I have found prayer really hard lately. I feel that I wore myself out praying for Travis, and while we accept the outcome, God did not answer my prayers for healing. So how do I pray for you? It's not that I am disillusioned with prayer but maybe just more realistic. I pray more to tell God I am confused and unsure. I pray that He will give you grace and courage through this. I realize there is no word, prayer, tone or emotion that will make a difference. God will do what He wants. As with Travis, many are asking God to heal you. Will a particular prayer, someone's prayer, be the one that gets through? I don't see it that way any longer. God is God. He will do what He wants for His glory and purpose. For me, prayer has been more about reflecting on that.

I love you,
Dad

My Dear Boy,

You came home this week on Monday. It was such a relief to see you free of tubes and lines and eating freely. Wow, you have a lot of catching up to do in the food department. You've had a good couple days since being home, even walking around the block with me.

Yesterday we got a super encouraging phone call from the oncologist. The bone fragment and lymph nodes taken at surgery show no sign of cancer. This is big. It means that to this point the only cancer detected was in the tumor that was removed during the operation. More tests are needed. In fact, as I am writing this, we are back at Children's Hospital awaiting a CT and bone scan. If these tests are negative, then your cancer is officially a level two: serious but very treatable. Of course you will still need chemo, they are telling us.

I wonder what script God is writing for us in all this. What will the story be six months from now, two years from now, seven years, twenty years? Do I want to know?

Several months ago a dear woman at church read my book, <u>Fires of Sorrow</u> [first edition to this book], and she told me she really enjoyed it. She then innocently asked me if I was planning on writing a sequel, as though what she had read was a mystery novel. I looked at her and simply replied, "I hope not to."

Is this the sequel? Your story? Last week in the hospital, Breanna was lying on the couch leaning on the shoulder of her best friend, Addie. Breezy, without moving, yelled over to me and said, "Dad, does this mean you're going to write another book?" I remember looking at you lying on the bed, tired, worn out, and seemingly emotional, when she said this. I noticed some muscles on your face twitching, and you began to cry softly and said, "Breanna, don't say that." Breezy felt really bad and said so. I quickly reassured her with a whisper that it was okay. I wondered then, but did not ask you, if you were thinking more about Travis at that moment than yourself.

I love how Breanna is being so open and vulnerable about your situation. She is strong as her name suggests: *strong and courageous*. You both have always been so close, and I can tell you are leaning on each other right now. I love watching how she's been growing spiritually in this last year, almost to prepare all of us through her strength. Two years ago, out of concern for her, I began to take the Wednesday lunch hour to pray and fast for her. I would write my prayers for her, and I plan on keeping that journal. I wonder if this trial is the answer to those prayers? When we ask that Jesus would strengthen our children and that they would grow in their faith, are we not asking that God spare them of pain? Isn't that the way we all grow? When we pray for our children, we need to be ready to accept how God answers those prayers. This sometimes occurs by Him testing our children.

I love you,
Dad

Chapter 35
A Turn for the Better

This was the last letter I wrote to Brett in my journal. Shortly after his diagnosis, I put together a CaringBridge account to give updates to people on his situation. It consisted of only several entries, and I stopped updating once his condition improved. Here are several of those entries.

Journal Entry by Mitch Schultz — June 15, 2006

We did not leave Children's until 5:30 last evening. I think we were too tired to feel any kind of joy over this being Brett's last treatment. He was so tired, and when we arrived home, you could see him beginning to wear out. He felt quite sick and went to bed around 8:30. Haven't seen him yet. We assume today will be a hard day for him. Do pray that his counts will remain high and that he will not respond with fever and severe loss of energy as he did last time.

Our house is a mess. While caring for Brett, we are also clearing out our house while watching World Cup soccer. (Actually, I watch the soccer while Elaine packs. Just kidding!) We have to be out by next Friday when the movers come to take our things to Franklin. We will stay at some friends' house who are away for the summer. Honestly, it will be like a vacation home. To think that we will not need to pack our last month here.

Journal Entry by Mitch Schultz — June 16, 2006

Brett slept most of yesterday and was sick a few times, but he had no fever, for which we are thankful. Today, he seems to have perked up and managed to watch some World Cup soccer with me. Right now he is watching Mouse Hunt and just had lunch. The house looks like a storage unit for all that the Schultz's own. What a mess! The more you clear out, the more you find you have. One more week, and we are out of here. Hard to believe.

Journal Entry by Mitch Schultz — June 19, 2006

Brett finally went outside today. We went on a five minute walk this evening and after that managed to kick a soccer ball together in the backyard. This is the first bit of activity he has had since his treatment last Wednesday. His spirits remain high despite the tiredness and having to put up with boxes and packing all around him. Seeing all the boxes in the house makes the move so much more real. Only four more days and we are out of this home, our home for the past five years. Come to think of it, this is the longest I have ever been in one house my entire life. WOW! Elaine and I long that our next move to Franklin will be the last one for a lonnnngggg time.

Journal Entry by Mitch Schultz — June 22, 2006

"What a difference a day makes," my mother used to say. (Actually I have no idea who said it. Hey, I just said it!) Yesterday was a huge day for Brett. In the morning, he went to be with a friend and ended up spending the rest of the day with him and two other buddies. When he arrived home and after we had supper, he had enough energy reserve left to KICK A SOCCER BALL WITH HIS DAD! All this in the spirit of the World Cup. In fact, in just a moment he is coming downstairs to share the space next to me to help cheer on the USA against Ghana. We are so pleased with how well Brett has done since this last treatment. Furthermore, yesterday we noticed THE HAIR IS GROWING BACK! Sorry Grandpa Schultz, that is something you never get to look forward to.

We have one day left in our home. The movers come tomorrow. Breanna left for Ecuador yesterday with our youth group. Last night, I went into her room and wept softly as I thought that this is no longer hers. So much to look forward to but so many memories to revisit. I tell Elaine that I attach a lot of memories to places. This comes with having lived in eight different countries in 45 years.

Journal Entry by Mitch Schultz — June 24, 2006

We are out of our house and staying at some friends' house who are away for the summer. What a beautiful place they have. It was hard to leave our house. Breanna is in Ecuador, and I wish we could have gone through the house together to say goodbye. Brett, Elaine and I did, and we wept and prayed in Brett's room. We thanked the Lord for the memories and for the people we have gotten to know in this house. We thanked Him for the roof over our head, for daily provision, and we thanked Him that He will provide for the seasons ahead. He is our ROCK, and we trust Him. He is a firm foundation and one in whom we can find great shelter. We can move a million times, and the true foundation remains the same.

Journal Entry by Mitch Schultz — June 27, 2006

Brett continues to do well. Blood drawn last Friday shows no drop in counts. His hair is slowly growing back. He is struggling with soreness and weakness in his legs and a very weak voice. We assume this is from the impact of the treatment on his system. We are comfortably settled at our temporary home and enjoying not packing and the view around us. I told Elaine last evening when I returned from work that it is like being on vacation. Hey, the ROCK is still holding us up.

Journal Entry by Mitch Schultz — June 29, 2006

Great day yesterday. Brett spent most of Monday at Church where kids are auditioning for the summer drama camp scheduled for the first week of August. Brett has a main part, and the gal in charge has rewritten his lines to include his story of surviving cancer. Last evening, we went to some friends' house for a bonfire. Brett's strength continues to improve daily.

Journal Entry by Mitch Schultz — July 7, 2006

Quick update. Brett was scanned all day today. This is the big day that we have been looking forward to in determining if all the cancer was removed. We meet with the oncologist on Tuesday for the results. Brett is doing so much better and is quite active now, playing with me and meeting with friends. We are very pleased with how he is doing.

Journal Entry by Mitch Schultz — July 11, 2006

GREAT NEWS! BRETT IS CLEAR! We sat waiting for the oncologist this morning, and when she walked in, she looked too serious for my liking. I had been expecting to hear that the scans from this past Friday would show "all clear," but I was also prepared if they didn't. She sat down and immediately said, "The scans look good." All four of us could have hugged her. We praise Jesus. He has been so good, so kind, and so faithful.

Brett will have his case turned over to the oncology department in Greenville, South Carolina. We will probably need to journey there once a month for a year. It's not a bad travel, only one and half hours.

Because of today's news, I don't expect to be updating this site for some time. I assume if there is different news on Brett in the months or years ahead, you will hear one way or another from us. Meanwhile, I sign off with a lightness in my spirit that I have not sensed since before this latest trial. I know this experience strengthens faith, but we have been tried. We move into a new place, a new home, and a new ministry with deeper confidence and greater love for our Lord Jesus. I am eager to preach on His goodness and to share His love and compassion with others who hurt. Elaine and I sense a special calling to come alongside the suffering and the grieving. As we heal further, we desire to serve our Lord and to walk on with Him no matter what the journey presents. There is no assurance that there will not be more trials. I expect there will. Yet, I love Him so much, and I praise Him that He has trusted us with this and that we have been given another opportunity to demonstrate our love and trust in Him. My prayer for you is that you will know Him, trust Him and serve Him. My prayer is that He will be your ROCK as He has been ours. - Mitch, Elaine, Breanna and Brett. We love you. I will keep checking this site for your letters to give to Brett.

Chapter 36
Settling, Finally!

We ended up moving to North Carolina just four months later than planned. Brett struggled for a year, both physically and emotionally. In the end, Breanna and Brett thrived with this move. Our family struggled to find a new, healthy place in all these trials, and I believe we finally did. Ironically, as our family strengthened, we were asked for the first time in my twenty-some years of ministry to now pastor a church "suffering from cancer," I jokingly told people. Maybe it's not funny that our family's experience with cancer prepared us well to care for this terminally ill body in North Carolina. We endured for seven years. Exhausted, we eventually sought outside intervention, and the decision was made for us to move on. And move on we all did. Elaine and I are now happily settled near a lake in Toccoa, Georgia where I enjoy serving as director of a ministry called Fruitful Vine Ministry. This ministry is designed to encourage, counsel and support those in ministry who are hurting.

We are thrilled to live just seven miles from Breanna, who is now married to Michael Kowalski. They have given us a precious granddaughter, Anora, who we spend time with three to four days a week. Brett has served as a Creative Producer with Student Life Camps in Birmingham, AL. Since leaving there in the summer of 2018, he's taken some bold steps to enter the acting and theater world, driven there by his love for Jesus. I asked him recently to tell me how his experience with cancer shaped him and this is what he said, "Cancer forced me into early spiritual maturity. It wasn't maturity I had asked for or even wanted. But thank God it was His choice for me and not mine, because that early maturity gave me the tools I needed to gain an eternal perspective. Since then, I have wanted nothing more than to show people how to have joy amidst trial. His timing was perfect then and is perfect now."

Chapter 37
Sorrow No More!

Elaine and I moved to England with our family with a simple but clear desire to do what we felt God was leading us to do. When we moved on to Wisconsin, and later to North Carolina and now to Georgia, that desire never diminished. Years earlier, we both had committed our lives to God to go wherever and to do whatever He wanted. We did not think that England was in desperate need for people like us or that, as Americans, we had something better to offer. Not at all. We just wanted to be in a place where we could make a difference and be of encouragement to people who might perhaps be disillusioned with Christianity. We wanted to help those who needed to better understand who God really is.

Our main responsibility in those early years was to pastor, but we loved the opportunity to become friends with many others in the community. We felt welcomed by them, and it did not take long to find ourselves a part of community life. We never pushed our faith on anyone. Our quiet desire has always been that our friends see a personal side of God and recognize a Christianity that is often not seen. This attitude toward God is often blurred by people's discontent or bad experiences with traditional Christianity. It has been our hope that our friends, regardless of whether or not they attend church, understand that God loves them and longs for them to become a part of His family.

What has happened to Elaine, Travis and Brett does not make us angry at God. Rather, the crises have drawn us closer to Him. I can speak for Elaine because I know her heart and the depth of her faith in God. There have been times recently when I asked her if all of this has made her bitter toward God. She is now finally able to communicate well, so her reply was weighted with a great deal of conviction. She replied, "Mitch, what good would that do?"

I have found that the alternative to acceptance and dependence on God is rejection of and independence from God, and it is not very attractive. Who in their right mind would prefer a broken relationship over a harmonious one? Imagine a wife saying to her husband, "Sorry, but I would prefer being mad at you and having a strain in our relationship." I have been tempted to treat God that way, but what good does it do to be mad at God? Isn't it when I hurt that I need Him the most? I think so.

I spent hours in the family room at Walton Hospital in England and the radiation center at Emory in Atlanta and years later at Children's Hospital in Milwaukee. I had many opportunities to listen to people's pain and anguish as they, too, awaited the recovery of their loved ones. I overheard many of those family members let off steam against God. Their comments often were directed my way when they discovered what I do and what I believe. For many of those families, what was happening to them cemented an opinion of God that was already in their hearts: *He is not loving, and He doesn't care.*

I listened patiently, but I also shared how God was extending His loving arms to me, and I was finding great comfort in His embrace. This has been a better option than being angry at God. In fact, being angry at God makes no more sense to me than does a child's taking out his anger on his father because the child has stubbed his toe while playing outdoors.

Early on in Travis's ordeal, I asked him if he was alright with all that he would have to face. His response showed me someone who preferred God's embrace to the distance of bitterness. "Yes Dad, it is alright, because God is in it!"

What is it that gives us and other Christians this perspective about suffering? I would like to offer two reasons why what happened to Elaine and Travis does not make us want to give up but rather motivates us to press on with God. One reason has to do with a *present relationship*; the other has to do with a *future promise*.

Years ago, I was tucking six-year-old Brett into bed. Just as I began to pray with him, he interrupted. "Daddy," he said, "I used to not like God very much!"

My reply was marked with some apprehension, unsure where he was going with this. "Why is that, Brett?" I asked.

"Because I couldn't see Him," was his simple reply.

I pressed further. "Do you mean that now you can see Him?"

"No, but now it doesn't matter."

Brett didn't intend to do so, but he hit the nail of Christianity on the head with this simple insight. To have a relationship with God does not require that we see God but rather that *we believe* what the Bible says about Him and respond by giving ourselves fully to Him. Yet, we cannot become a Christian or enter this new relationship unless we first acknowledge that we are separated from Him by that big problem called sin.

The Bible describes a gulf that exists between man and God. Man, despite his attempts to bridge that gulf, remains separated from God. This gulf was bridged when Jesus laid His life across that chasm. To have this relationship with God requires a simple step on our part – that we come to God through Jesus. We must admit that we are utterly helpless and sinful and unable to save ourselves on our own. Jesus, being God, came to live in our world as the God Man, the perfect man who alone lived the kind of life, the perfect life approved by God. His death on our behalf became the only basis by which we can come to God. By confessing our sins, repenting of those sins and acknowledging that on the cross Jesus took on Himself the punishment we deserve, we are saved.

When Travis was just four, he joined a bigger and more lasting family. He asked Jesus to wash him of the sin with which he was born. This act proved to be a life-changing decision that prepared Travis to face anything. This relationship with Jesus is what also gave Travis an eagerness in dying because he knew who he would finally see face to face beyond the grave. It is also that same faith that gives Brett the deep resolve to do all he does for the glory of God.

Had I not become a member of God's family, I could not possibly accept such pain and suffering as described in this book. I would find myself doubting God and even, as many people do, rebelling against Him. You've no doubt heard that common statement, "How can a loving God allow such a thing?" To Elaine and me, a friendship with Jesus has always come before physical or personal security. When bad things happen, this friendship does not change. Instead, it grows stronger. A portion from the Bible sketches a beautiful portrait of this bond: "For I am convinced that neither death nor life, neither angels nor demons, neither the present nor the future, nor any powers, neither height nor depth, nor anything else in all creation, will be able to separate us from the love of God that is in Christ Jesus our Lord" (Rom. 8:38-39).

Christians often say that they draw closer to God in hardship. To them, what matters more than health or personal security is a friendship with Jesus. So when bad things do happen, we need that friendship far more than when things are going well. I'll take His embrace rather than the distance that comes from being angry at Him.

I recently read a book about a missionary working in Indonesia who was interned by the Japanese for five years during World War II. Her first anguish in this trial was to be separated from her husband when he and the other men were taken to another camp. She had no word of him for more than a year until one day someone informed her that he had died three months earlier. She was crushed. She would have collapsed and given up all desire to live, had it not been for her deep conviction that one day she would be reunited with him and, more importantly, with her Lord Jesus. In 2004, Darlene Deibler, in her late eighties, had all her hopes realized when she passed on to join her husband and to finally meet her Savior.

It is this hope of life after death, the promise that God gives us in the Bible, that keeps my family going in the hardest of times. Christians anchor to the promise that death is not the end and that there is far more when it is all over on Earth. It is that sort of hope that enables all Christians to say "it's okay" when they lose a loved one, and "it will all work out for the better in the end" when things here don't go their way. This doesn't mean that Christians don't experience anguish and deep pain. They are vulnerable like everyone else. It is their hope in something more, however, that helps them live through the pain. We call this endurance.

Jeremiah, the Old Testament prophet, promised a day when we will be free of all sorrow. I cling to this promise: "They will be like a well-watered garden, and they will sorrow no more" (Jer. 31:12).

This is what keeps me going and what gives me hope. I admit right now that things are not what I planned for us. I can honestly say that I don't like it very much. I would love to be able to snap my fingers and see Elaine fully restored and have Travis back at my side. However, there are some things that I cannot change. But I live for that day when it will be alright again – and even better than we ever had it before. Absorb this image from the Bible for just a moment: "And I heard a voice from the throne saying, 'Now the dwelling of God is with men, and he will live with them. They will be his people, and God himself will be with them and be their God. He will wipe every tear from their eyes. There will be no more death or mourning or crying or pain, for the old order of things has passed away'" (Rev. 21:3-4).

This future promise is available only to those who have put their trust in Jesus. It makes sense to me that people who ignore Jesus in this life should not expect much of a break after this life. Elaine and I have had one simple desire from all of our friendships during the years we have lived in England and America. This desire is that *we will be able to enjoy eternity together.*

Interestingly, the lady's question (asking if I would ever write a sequel) had a prophetic ring to it. I guess this is that sequel. I hope this edition, whether you're reading it for the first time or reading it again with this update, would encourage you in your faith. I hope it encourages you to keep trusting Jesus in whatever fires of sorrow God has asked you to walk through or maybe, for the first time, to put your trust in Him. By the time you close this book, I want you to be able to say what Elaine often says, "Life stinks, but Jesus is so good!"

I do hope that the aroma of our faith, fueled by the stinging flames of our trials, would add to your desire to see your life given in worship to God.

What better way for me to end this than to join David in saying, "It was good for me to be afflicted so that I might learn your decrees. The law from your mouth is more precious to me than thousands of pieces of silver and gold" (Psalm 119:71-72).

MY FAVORITE MEMORIES ARE OF TRAVIS SMILING

**TRAVIS DOING WHAT HE LOVED BEST:
PLAYING SOCCER**

TRAVIS HOLDING THE FA CUP WON BY HIS FAVORITE TEAM, EVERTON, IN 1995

TRAVIS, BRETT AND BREANNA TWO MONTHS BEFORE HIS PASSING

FAMILY PICTURE AFTER TRAVIS COMPLETED RADIATION TREATMENT

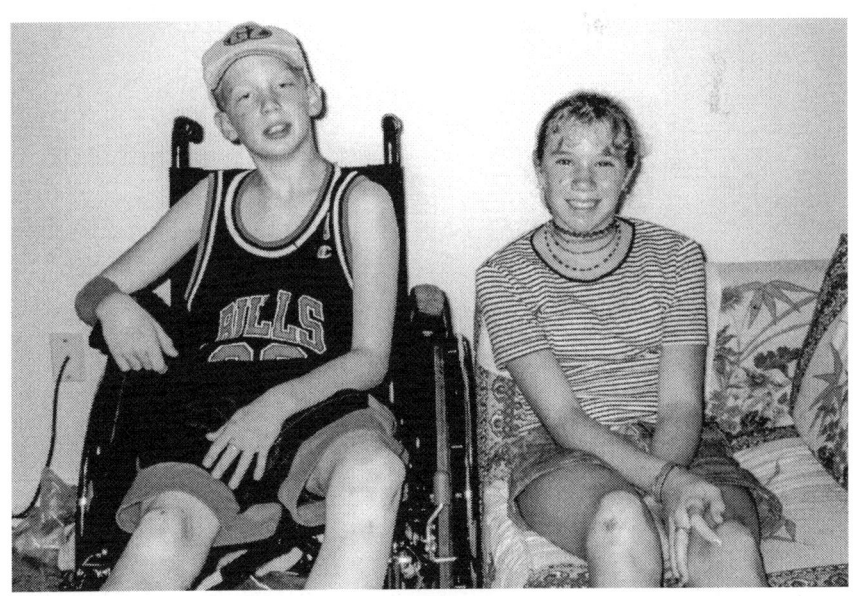

TRAVIS WITH HIS BEST FRIEND AND COUSIN MELANIE

FAMILY VACATION ONE YEAR AFTER BRETT'S CANCER

ELAINE AND BRETT (NOW 25) IN LOUISVILLE, KY

**BRETT'S FORMAL HEADSHOT FOR
ACTING AUDITIONS**

Also by Mitch A. Schultz

DID I SAY THE RIGHT THING?

Mitch Schultz knows what it is to wonder what to say to someone mourning the loss of a loved one. He also knows what it's like to say something to a mourner and afterward want to kick yourself. If you've had either experience, he gets you. But more than that, he has endured loss and knows firsthand what it's like to be the one grieving. Out of his experience he provides insight and suggestions that will help you avoid having to ask, "Did I say the right thing?" This book will help you minister wisely, compassionately, and effectively to those who grieve. (Available on Amazon and Regular Baptist Press - www.regularbaptistpress.org)

THE WHISPER; (Book One of the Andre Michael Lansing Novel Series)

Pastor Andre Michael Lansing still struggles with the loss of his daughter to a car accident. He and his wife, Sophia, have trouble letting go of their grief and decide that a new start in a new city may be for the best. They move to Lowensville, TN where Andre works hard to serve his church and his congregation. But an abusive husband has the good pastor in his sights. The man, Whitlock, manipulates his wife into making false allegations of sexual indecency toward Andre, and the situation escalates when members of Andre's church start to believe the couple's claims. The  pressure is too much for Andre, and he runs—from Lowensville, and from God Himself. Andre struggles through his feelings of fear, anger, and doubt—emotions that push him to make irrational decisions. Andre refuses to turn back to God. Like Jonah, however, in his flight, he finds his way back to God, who brings three men into his life and uses them to help Andre work through the obstacles that have kept him from truly knowing God. The pastor learns that sometimes we must be completely broken in order to hear the quiet whisper of the Lord.—The Reverend Doctor Dennis R. Maynard, episkopols.com, popular author of When Sheep Attack! (Available on Amazon)

THE GUARDIANS: A Story of Innocence and Betrayal (Book Two of the Andre Michael Lansing Novel Series)

Was Carson wrong to marry Gentiva? From the moment he took his first pastorate in the mountains of North Carolina, he remained resolute in his commitment. Betrayed and unknowingly the subject of a madman's (from The Whisper) obsession to seek revenge, Carson's world held together only by the unconditional support of his elders (his guardians) and the relentless faithfulness of his Savior. This story of innocence, betrayal and near personal and spiritual collapse makes it practically impossible to read this book in more than two sittings. In a surprising series of twists and turns, The Guardians challenges many of our assumptions of what it really means to trust God through the people he places in our lives. (Available on Amazon)

Made in the USA
Columbia, SC
27 January 2020